FREEDOM!

FROM BELOW

The Struggle for Trade Unions in South Africa

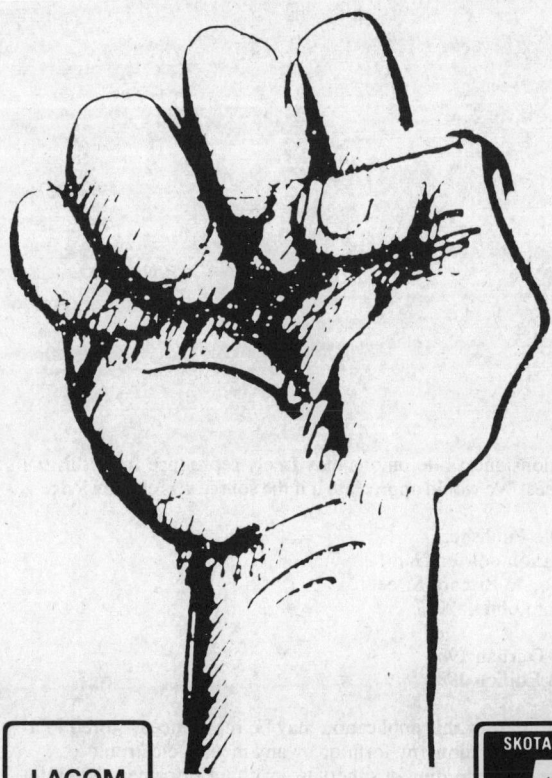

LACOM
A
Project
of
Sached

SKOTAVILLE

EDUCATIONAL DIVISION

Throughout this book we use racial terms created by the bosses and the government. This is not because we accept these terms, but because in our country so many laws control the actions of 'different races'. We use the terms Indian, Coloured, African and White. When we use the word 'Black', we are referring to Indians, Coloureds and Africans together.

Community organisations and trade unions may freely reproduce from this book for educational purposes. We would appreciate it if the source was acknowledged.

Published by Skotaville Publishers
(Incorporated Association not for Gain)
307 Hampstead House, 46 Biccard Street,
P.O. Box 32483, Braamfontein 2017

ISBN 0 947479 02 3

Printed and bound by Blackshaws (Pty) Ltd, Johannesburg and Cape Town.

Comrades!

My name is Thami and I work in a factory in Pinetown near Durban. At Pinetown, we have a lot of factories and the working class is well organised into trade unions. But, this was not always so.

I remember the strikes which broke out in Durban in 1973. I didn't go on strike then. I was sure that those workers would lose their jobs.

But then in about 1975, some workers in our factory began to talk about organising a union. Again, I said no, that was not for me. All I wanted to do was my job and get my pay at the end of the week.

But these workers carried on organising anyway. They formed a shop stewards' steering committee. And after they had signed up many members, they held elections for shop stewards.

It was then that I really began to understand what the union was about. Together it would be easier to get our rights from the bosses. Also, if we elected our leaders in our department, then we could control that person. We could make sure that our shop steward represented our position to the bosses clearly.

Then I signed up and started thinking about trade unions more carefully. Had there always been trade unions in South Africa? How were these unions organised? What role did African workers play in these unions? I asked myself many questions.

Eventually I decided that the only way to find answers was to go and find out for myself.

The only way I could do this was to read. I contacted my union organiser who gave me plenty of books and articles about trade unions. But these articles and books were written by people at universities. They were very difficult to understand.

For many years I just read. But then I thought that all this information was being hidden from workers. It needed to be written again, so that it is useful for workers who want to understand the history of trade unions.

That is how this book started. It has turned out to be very long, but this is only because of the long history of working class struggles in South Africa.

I am sure that some people who read this book will find some problems. I couldn't include every single struggle that workers organised. That would take many books and many years. Anyway, most of our struggles haven't even been written about.

This is a big problem. We have to learn to write our own history. Otherwise, no one will ever really understand how we have struggled. What is worse, if we don't write about the battles we are fighting now, the job of writing will stay with people from the universities. No one will know what really happened in the factory, in the shop stewards' council and in the townships.

You will find that the book is broken into many chapters. The chapters each tell a story and can be read on their own, one by one. On the first page of every chapter you will see a summary which tells you what the chapter is about.

Whatever you do, comrades, read the book. Read it slowly if you like. Take many months. Read it together with other comrades in a study group and discuss the issues which each chapter talks about. In this way, you will look at some of the issues and develop your own point of view.

Comrades this is your book, use it!

Contents

ABBREVIATIONS

AAC — All Africa Convention

AAWU — African Allied Workers Union

ABWU — Amalgamated Black Workers Union

ACTWUSA — Amalgamated Clothing and Textile Workers Union

ACWU — African Clothing Workers Union

AFCWU — African Food and Canning Workers Union

AFGWU — African General Workers Union

AGPWU — African Gas and Power Workers Union

AME — Amalgamated Engineering Union

AMWU — African Mineworkers Union

ANC — African National Congress

APDUSA — African Peoples Democratic Union of South Africa

APO — African Peoples Organisation

AZACTU — Azanian Confederation of Trade Unions

AZAPO — Azanian Peoples Organisation

AZASM — Azanian Students Movement

AZAYO — Azanian Youth Organisation

BAMCWU — Black Allied Mining and Construction Workers Union

BAWU — Black Allied Workers Union

BCWU — Brushes and Cleaners Workers Union

BEEWU — Black Electronics and Electrical Workers Union

BCAWU — Building Construction and Allied Workers Union

BCAWU — Brick, Clay and Allied Workers Union

BDWA — Black Domestic Workers Association

BIFAWU — Banking Insurance and Finance Assurance Workers Union

BLAGWU — Black General Workers Union

BLATU — Black Laundry Trade Unions

BMWU — The Black Municipal Workers Union

BPC — Black Peoples Convention

BWP — Black Workers Project

CAL — Cape Action League

CAWU — Construction and Allied Workers Union

CCATU — Co-ordinating Committee of African Trade Unions

CCAWUSA — Commercial, Catering and Allied Workers Union

CCOBTU — Consultative Committee of Black Trade Unions

CCSATU — Co-ordinating Council of South African Trade Unions

CDWU — Commercial Distributive Workers Union

CFLU — Cape Federation of Labour Unions

CIWW — Council of Industrial Workers of the Witwatersrand

CNETU — Council for Non-European Trade Unions

COSAS — Congress of South African Students

COSATU — Congress of South African Trade Unions

CSAWU — Cleaning Services and Allied Workers Union

CTMWA — Cape Town Muncipal Workers Association

CUSA — Council of Unions of South Africa

CWIU — Chemical Workers Industrial Union

DIMES — Durban Indian Municipal Employees Association

DWASA — Domestic Workers Association of South Africa

EAWU — Engineering and Allied Workers Union

EAWTUSA — Electrical and Allied Workers Trade Union of South Africa

FAWU — Food and Allied Workers Union

FBWU — Food and Beverage Workers Union

FCWU — Food and Canning Workers Union

FMBWU — Furniture, Mattress and Bedding Workers Union

FNETU — South African Federation of Non-European Trade Unions

FOFATUSA — Federation of Free African Trade Unions

FOSATU — Federation of South African Trade Unions

FPAWU — Farm, Plantation and Allied Workers Union

FWIU — Furniture Workers Industrial Union

GAWU — General and Allied Workers Union

GAWU — Glass and Allied Workers Union

GFWBF — General Factory Workers Benefit Fund

GWU — Garment Workers Union

GWU — General Workers Union

GWUSA — General Workers Union of South Africa

HAWU — Health and Allied Workers Union

HOTELICA — Hotel, Liquor, Catering and Allied Workers Union

IAS — Industrial Aid Society

IAWUSA — Insurance and Assurance Workers Union of South Africa

ICFTU — International Confederation of Free Trade Unions

ICU — Industrial and Commercial Workers Union

IMS — Iron Moulders Society

ISATA — South African Iron and Steel Trades Association

IWA — Industrial Workers of Africa

JCATU — Joint Committee of African Trade Unions

JGU — Jewellers and Goldsmiths Union

LDCWA — Laundry, Dry Cleaning and Dye Workers Association

MACWUSA — Motor Assembly and Component Workers Union

MAWU — Metal and Allied Workers Union

MGWUSA — Municipal and General Workers Union of South Africa

MWU — Milling Workers Union

MWU — Mineworkers Union

MWUSA — Municipal Workers Union of South Africa

NAAWU — National Automobile and Allied Workers Union

NAPAWU — National Post Office and Allied Workers Union

NEHAWU — National Education Health and Allied Workers Union

NEUSA — National Education Union of South Africa

NF — National Forum

NFATU — Natal Federation of African Trade Unions

NFW — National Federation of Workers

NGWU — National General Workers Union

NIC — Natal Indian Congress

NISMAWU — National Iron, Steel, Metal Workers Union

NMCA — Native Mine Clerks Association

NOW — Natal Organisation of Women

NUCW — National Union of Clothing Workers

NUDW — National Union of Distributive Workers

NUF — National Union of Farmworkers

NULCDW — National Union of Laundry, Cleaning and Dyeing Workers

NUM — National Union of Mineworkers

NUMSA — National Union of Metalworkers of South Africa

NUMARWOSA — National Union of Motor and Rubber Workers of South Africa

NUSAS — National Union of South African Students

NUTW — National Union of Textile Workers

NUWSA — National Union of Workers of South Africa

NUWSAW — National Union of Wine, Spirit and Allied Workers

NWC — Natal Workers Congress

OVGWU — The Orange Vaal General Workers Union

PEBCO — Port Elizabeth Black Civic Organisation

PEWO — Port Elizabeth Women's Organisation

PWAWU — Paper Wood and Allied Workers Union

PTU — Progressive Group of Trade Unions

RAWU — Retail and Allied Workers Union

SAAWU — South African Allied Workers Union

SACCOLA — South African Employers Consultative Committee on Labour Affairs

SACOD — South African Congress of Democrats

SACL — South African Confederation of Labour

SACP — South African Communist Party

SACTU — South African Congress of Trade Unions

SACWU — South African Chemical Workers Union

SADWA — South African Domestic Workers Association

SADWU — South African Domestic Workers Union

SAFTU — South African Federation of Trade Unions

SAIC — South African Indian Congress

SAIF — South African Industrial Federation

SAMWU — South African Mineworkers Union

SARHWU — South African Railways and Harbour Workers Union

SASO — South African Students Organisation

SASTAWU — South African Scooter Transport and Allied Workers Union

SATAWU — South African Textile and Allied Workers Union

SATU — South African Typographical Union

SATWU — South African Transport Workers Union

SATWU — South African Tin Workers Union

SEAWU — Steel, Engineering and Allied Workers Union

SATUC — South African Trade Union Council

SFAWU — Sweet, Food and Allied Workers Union

TAWU — Transport and Allied Workers Union

TCNETU — Transvaal Council for Non-European Trade Unions

TGWU — Transport and General Workers Union

TUACC — Trade Union Advisory Co-ordinating Committee

TUCSA — Trade Union Council of South Africa

TWIU — Textile Workers Industrial Union

UAMAWU — United African Motor and Allied Workers Union

UAW — United Automobile Workers

UDF — United Democratic Front

UMMAWOSA — United Mining, Metal and Allied Workers of South Africa

UTP — Urban Training Project

WPFLU — Western Province Federation of Labour Unions

WPWAB — Western Province Workers Advice Bureau

WPGWU — Western Province General Workers Union

WTA — Witwatersrand Taylors Association

WWU — Women Workers Union

Chapter One
The Search for Workers:
1800 – 1920s

A class of workers – people who sell their labour to survive – has to be built for capitalism to survive. Without workers, there can be no production and no profits.

The early days of capitalism in South Africa were built largely around trade and commercial agriculture.

To do this, the White settlers with the support of Britain and Holland fought for control of the land and labour in southern Africa.

Early societies in Southern Africa resisted the power of White settlers and British and Dutch imperialism. These societies established a tradition of resistance to exploitation and repression. The South African working class has continued to resist and organise in this tradition.

This chapter looks at the early years of capitalism and at some of the struggles against exploitation and repression.

It is broken into the following sections:

1. **Early Societies in Southern Africa**

2. **White Settler Conquest – The Struggle for Land**

3. **The Roots of Capitalism – Trade and Commercial Agriculture**

4. **The Move to Wage Labour**

5. **The Search for Workers – Indentured Labour on the Sugar Farms**

6. **Resistance on the Sugar Farms**

7. **Smashing the South African Peasantry – The Way Forward for Capitalism**

1. Early Societies in Southern Africa

There have been people living in different parts of southern Africa since the birth of Christ. The activities of these societies are difficult to trace. But what has become clear is that there were people farming off the land from at least 400 AD and producing food and other goods for their survival.

Before 1870 most Africans, for example, the Swazi, Zulu, Xhosa, Ndebele, Pedi, Venda, Basotho lived in independent chiefdoms. There were also a number of chiefdoms like the Pondo, around the area of what is now called the Eastern Cape, Ciskei and Transkei.

It was these, often strong and well established societies, which the White settlers faced when they came to conquer southern Africa.

These societies grew crops, herded cattle and hunted wild animals. Some of these early societies mined metals like iron ore and copper, and made clay pottery. They made tools (like hoes and knives), things for the household (like mats and buckets) and weapons (like spears and shields).

There was a lot of contact between these different chiefdoms. They exchanged goods and traded with each other. Some societies in southern Africa sent trading parties as far as the north-east African coast. These people bartered with Arabs who came in ships to the coast.

But there was conflict between and within these African societies. Sometimes wars were fought over the ownership of land and cattle. The population of these chiefdoms grew. When they moved to new land, they found other people were living there already.

So chiefdoms began to fight for more land. These wars over land and resources changed the way that these societies were organised to produce.

People survived in southern Africa by farming the land and producing goods to survive.

Chiefdoms began organising in different ways. They formed bigger armies of young men. The chief became more powerful. He had greater control over what was produced by his people. He also usually had some control over the surplus labour* of his people.

surplus labour – here this means that the chief had some control over the kinds of jobs and work that people did.

The stronger chiefdoms were able to take over the land of other chiefdoms by force. In this way large chiefdoms were formed. Here power was centralised in the hands of fewer people – the chief and his headmen. They had greater control over the trade of ivory, guns and even slaves.

New chiefdoms came into being in southern and central Africa. It was during this time that the Zulu, the Basotho and Ndebele chiefdoms were formed.

These struggles for scarce resources were not only the result of conflict between different chiefdoms.

14

When the Dutch and British settlers arrived, battles were fought from the start. This was only the beginning of the bloody and violent process of exploitation and oppression that was to develop throughout the region of southern Africa.

The rich history of the people of South Africa before the development of capitalism still has to be fully written. What is clear is that before the arrival of White settlers there was a thriving political and economic system in the region which is now called South Africa.

In the years which followed, this system was violently overthrown in the capitalists' hungry search for profits.

2. White Settler Conquest – The Struggle for Land

The first contact between White settlers and the people living in southern Africa was filled with conflict. Between 1600 and 1677 many wars were fought between the Khoisan, who lived around the Cape, and the Dutch settlers. In 1600 there had been about 200 000 Khoisan living in the area – by 1799 only 20 000 were still alive!

In the early 1600s ships from Europe first started calling at the Cape of Good Hope (Cape Town) to pick up fresh water and food supplies. The Europeans traded with the Khoisan who were staying in this area. They gave the Khoisan beads, metals, liquor and dagga (from India) in exchange for cattle, sheep, ivory, ostrich feathers and shells.

In 1652, the Dutch East India Company (DEIC) decided to set up a permanent station at the Cape of Good Hope, so that their ships could stop for fresh water and food supplies. They needed these supplies because they had to travel long distances to trade in India and the Far East.

Soon more Dutch settlers came to settle at the Cape. A Dutch Colony* was set up. It was called the Cape Colony.

colony – a country which is ruled politically and economically by a more powerful country. This often happened when these powerful countries needed to expand their markets.

Dutch settlers started to herd cattle and grow crops. But to do this they needed land for farms and ranches. The land around the trading station was controlled by the Khoisan.

If the Dutch wanted to farm, they would have to take land away from the Khoisan and they did not worry about using force to do this.

But because most people in the area were still living off the land, the Dutch were forced to import slaves to work for them. Many of these slaves came from West Africa. Other Dutch farmers used the labour of dispossessed* Khoisan. They did not receive a wage for doing this work, but were given food, brandy and shelter.

dispossessed – people whose land was taken away, and way of life destroyed.

In 1806, Britain captured the Cape Colony from the Dutch. It was only after this, that very large numbers of White settlers came to live in southern Africa.

After the British took over the Cape Colony, many of the Dutch settlers left. They did not want to be under British rule. They moved inland away from the Cape Colony, to the Eastern Cape, Natal, Transvaal and the Orange Free State. They were known as the 'trekboers'.

British settlers also arrived in Natal and the East Cape in the 1820s. They established a port in Port Natal (Durban), and at Port Elizabeth.

The settlers traded with African chiefdoms in the area. There had always been trade in this region of Africa, but now many European traders travelled from the Cape Colony into the interior to trade with different chiefdoms. The chiefs were able to use this trade to increase their power in the chiefdoms.

African chiefdoms fought bitter battles against the Boers but they were eventually defeated because they did not have guns and other resources.

Once the Boers began to move inland, wars broke out over land between the settlers and the African chiefdoms. At first there were small battles between groups of settlers and chiefdoms. Sometimes different chiefdoms would unite against the settlers. Sometimes some chiefdoms would assist the settlers to defeat other chiefdoms.

These wars were a bitter struggle for the control and ownership of land.

Well, for most of the 1800s, Africans and White settlers in southern Africa fought bloody wars. These wars were over the control and ownership of land. This was because land was the most important thing needed for survival at this time.

The British government sent large armies with guns and cannons. This military strength put the settlers in a powerful position. It allowed them take over large areas of land.

The White settlers began to farm this land. Commercial agriculture for profits was started. Capitalism was forced on southern Africa!

---

3. The Roots of Capitalism – Trade and Commercial Agriculture

---

World trade expanded and so the demands of ships passing the Cape for food and drink grew. This trade laid the foundations for the growth of commercial agriculture*.

commercial agriculture – farming on a large scale to sell goods for profit.

Most people living in southern Africa were subsistence farmers. They planted crops and kept cattle to survive. But, commercial agriculture was very different from subsistence agriculture*.

subsistence agriculture – growing only enough food and goods for yourself and your family or your immediate dependants.

The port at Cape Town meant that White agriculture was geared for exports from the start. Wine was made from grapes and other food was planted to be sold to passing ships. Farmers at the Cape also started wool farming.

This early commercial agriculture at the Cape was based on slavery. Slaves herded the cattle and sheep and worked in the wheat fields and vineyards.

In Natal, the British had set up a port which was used as a trading station. In the Transvaal and Orange Free State the Boers, like the African farmers, were mainly subsistence farmers.

By 1880 the development of ports and trade had had a large effect on the region.

Commercial farming grew in Natal. Sugar became a more important export than ivory and hides. Britain's industries needed wool and sugar at this time and, Natal supplied ivory, hides, wool, sugar and wattle to Britain.

The arrival of settlers and their conquest of land violently changed the political and economic system in the southern African region. By the late 1800s, a firm basis had been laid for trade and commercial agriculture.

With the destruction of independent chiefdoms and the dispossession of land, capitalism now had room to start its growth. But, capitalism was still not strong, nor was the working class very big.

4. The Move to Wage Labour

In the 1850s, workers who were paid a money wage for their work started being used on a large scale. It was at this time, that we begin to see the emergence of a class of workers.

By the 1850s, there were already many farm workers in the commercial farming areas of the Western and Eastern Cape. There are many reasons for this:

- The Xhosa, who lived mainly in the South East and Western Cape had suffered a number of defeats in the hands of the Boer and British colonists. This resulted in large scale land and cattle dispossession.

- In their desperation they looked to their religious leadership for guidance and were advised to destroy their cattle and crops as a way of resisting colonisation.

- By 1859 about 30 000 Xhosa people were already in the Cape Colony looking for work or working and they were immediately placed in three to five year contracts in the Colony.

- There were also other workers in the Cape. Although slavery in the Cape Colony was abolished in 1838, former slaves and their children worked to survive.

From the 1850s onwards, greater parts of the land were brought under agricultural production by White settler farmers. This increased the demand for wage labour. Small towns in the Eastern Cape and the growing ports

of East London, Port Elizabeth and Cape Town all needed labour.

The South African working class was born. But it was a long and painful birth. From the beginning this class resisted the power of capitalism and imperialism.*

imperialism – the military, economic and political power that one country uses against the people of another country to exploit their land and labour.

- Between 1854 and 1857 dock workers went on strike for higher wages in Cape Town, Port Elizabeth and East London.

- In 1858, 200 African workers left their jobs at Kowie Food.

- Between 1860 and 1870 there were a number of strikes by African workers on the railways and other public works.

Decades of war, destruction and land dispossession forced the peoples of South Africa to look for work in the small towns and cities and on the farms. The Cape Colony was forced to implement taxes as early as 1857 to force people to look for work and money.

In Natal however, the farmers still faced major problems. Here between 1860 and 1911, sugar and wattle farmers were forced to bring over 150 000 workers from India to work on their farms!

By the 1860s, the different ports and small towns in the Western and Eastern Cape, and commercial agriculture had begun to employ wage labour. But the South African working class was still small.

The early days of capitalism – workers on a commercial farm.

5. The Search for Workers – Indentured Labour on the Sugar Farms

By the 1800s, the ability of chiefdoms to resist the move to wage labour differed from region to region. The Zulu kingdom near the Natal Colony was one chiefdom which was at first able to resist these pressures.

Most of the people living in Natal at this time were part of the Zulu kingdom. They had not been driven off the land although some laws had been passed to control Zulus and encourage wage labour. The Zulu kingdom was not finally defeated in battle until 1879, and was able to maintain some independence from the colonial government.

By the mid-1800s the sugar and wattle farmers in Natal had a number of problems. If their farms were to grow and expand they needed workers. The British government stepped in to help....

Workers cutting sugar cane in the 1850s

indenture – when people from one country work for capitalists in another country under contract for a period of time.

The British government brought people from India for a period of indenture*. Britain was the most powerful imperialist colonial power at this time and ruled with a strong navy and army. India was under British colonial rule.

These workers had to sign a contract to say that they would work for a period of five years. After this period was up they had a choice.

They could either renew their contract for a further five years, or return to India.

At the end of their second term of contract – which was also five years – workers again were given a number of 'choices'.

They could again renew their contracts, return to India, or buy themselves out of indenture and stay in Natal by paying three pounds to the British colonial government.

Working conditions were appalling

On some farms, workers worked for a minimum of twelve hours a day, and sometimes even up to seventeen or eighteen hours. During certain periods of the year, whole families had to do work on the farm.

Workers were housed in closed compounds under the direct control of farm managers. Conditions were unhealthy and workers often suffered from incurable diseases.

Many farms were run by an overseer or farm manager assisted by *sirdars* ('boss-boys'). They were the direct link between the workers and the owners.

The sirdars were given higher wages and other privileges, including the use of a *sjambok!*

The indentured labour of the 1800s was a very effective way of getting cheap labour for the sugar plantations. Sugar, after maize, became the most important crop for the whole of Natal.

It was on the back of cheap indentured labour that the sugar farmers built their empires of profit. Harsh working and living conditions and strict controls made worker organisation very difficult. But workers' resistance could not be killed!

6. Resistance on the Sugar Farms

In the early years of the sugar plantations, worker resistance was usually on an individual basis and unorganised. Workers who left a farm together in a group would have to pay fines if they were caught.

Group protests were few and low-key. They took the form of simple complaints to the Protector* who was appointed by the British colonial government in Natal. The Protector was supposed to look after the conditions of Indian indentured workers.

Protector – an official of the British colonial government.

There were not many strikes. Between 1900 and 1910 only about 4% of the indentured population went on strike. Workers also destroyed estate property.

Sometimes resistance took the form of malingering (pretending to be sick), absenteeism and desertion. The suicide rate amongst workers on the farms was high. This was often the only way some workers could resist their exploitation.

The growing working class on the farms in the Cape and Natal Colonies gave capitalism a great boost. Indentured labour helped solve the farmers' problems in Natal. But, it could not solve the capitalists' labour problems for the whole of southern Africa. Even in Natal farmers still had many problems.

The ruling classes* still faced major problems.

This was especially because many African farmers were still living on the land. They were often better farmers than the White settlers.

The White settlers defeated many chiefdoms

ruling classes – the group of people who control economic, political and military power in a country.

militarily. But to get rid of competition in agriculture, they had to smash the peasantry. *

peasantry – people who have some control over a small piece of land and try to live by farming that land.

7. Smashing the South African Peasantry – The Way Forward for Capitalism

The process of turning African subsistence farmers into peasants was speeded up through taxes. Africans had to pay a hut tax as well as a poll tax for every man over eighteen years. These taxes had to be paid in money. Subsistence farmers found that they had to produce a surplus* to sell for money to pay their taxes.

surplus – over and above what is needed.

After diamonds were mined for profit in 1867 and gold in 1886, towns began to grow, especially in the Transvaal. This increased the demand for agricultural products. Many African peasants began to produce more crops to sell to this growing market.

A successful African peasant in Groutville, Natal. He was one of many of the successful farmers who sold food to the growing towns.

Who were these peasants?

A peasant is someone who has access to a piece of land and uses their own labour as well as their family's labour to farm.

A peasant may also sell a portion of what is produced. This money is used to pay taxes, rents, and other fees that are imposed in an economic and political system outside peasant farming.

But, by the middle of the 1800s, not all African farmers owned or farmed land in the same way. Some were squatter peasants, sharecroppers, labour tenants or farmed on mission owned land.

merchants – people who live by trading and making a profit.

- Squatter peasants – Squatter peasants rented land owned by merchants*, land companies and land speculators (i.e. people who made money by buying and selling land at a higher price) and the colonial government in Natal and the Cape. The African farmers would sell their surplus to pay their rent.

- Sharecroppers – Some African farmers were tenants on White farms. They had an agreement with the farmer to plough and plant the land and would then share some of the crops with the farmer.

- Labour tenants – Labour tenants were given a piece of land to farm on condition they and their family worked on the White farmer's land at certain times of the year.

mission stations – church-owned land.

technology – here this word means advanced farming equipment and methods to increase production.

- Mission land – The mission stations* provided some land for Africans who had been dispossessed. At these stations, African farmers were introduced to new technology* which speeded up production. Many successful peasants farmed on the mission stations in the Cape and Natal as well as in the Transvaal.

At first the African farmers had advantages over the settler farmers. They had a much longer experience and knowledge of the climates, soils, animal life and vegetation found in the different parts of South Africa.

The White settlers had difficulty in adjusting to the soil and the climate of South Africa. Many of the farming implements and types of seeds that they imported were unsuitable for the South African soil and climate. The White farmers also needed labour to work on their farms.

On the other hand, African farmers worked with their family and sometimes friends. From about 1850 to 1900, African peasants were the largest and most successful producers of maize and sorghum in the colonies and Boer Republics.

But this did not last for long. New ports gave commercial agriculture a big boost. Now that their markets could expand, White farmers needed plenty of cheap labour on their farms. To get this, they first had to smash competition from the African peasants.

In the Boer Republics, the farmers asked the government to help them to get labour. Farmers in the Cape and Natal put pressure on the colonial governments to help them to get labour.

A number of laws were passed by the governments of the different provinces to try and turn African peasants and peasant squatters into workers.

- Locations Acts of 1869, 1876 and 1884 – These acts passed in the Cape Colony cut the number of squatters and rent-paying tenants on White farms. Farmers were fined unless they used wage labour.

- In the Transvaal, laws were passed in 1895 and again in 1911 and 1912 to try and cut down the number of squatters on White farms.

By the 1900s it was becoming clear that there was a need for a uniform policy by the ruling classes to control the movement and supply of workers in southern Africa.

In 1910 the two colonial governments in Natal and the Cape held a National Convention with the Boer Republics. At this National Convention, the Union of South Africa was formed. A parliament in South Africa passed laws for the whole country.

This parliament was for Whites. But a few Blacks in the Cape and Natal could also vote. With one government for the whole of South Africa, it became much easier to pass laws which could control the movement of labour.

In 1913 a law was passed for the whole of South Africa. This law said that no Whites could buy land in Black areas, and no Blacks could buy land in White areas.

The law also set aside only about 13% of the land in South Africa for Blacks. The areas where Blacks were to stay were called reserves. The size of the land that each family in the reserves was allowed to own was small. It could not be increased.

The law also made squatting a crime. Many squatters were turned into labour tenants. Thousands of peasants and their families were turned off the land by farmers who were afraid of being fined. They had to take their cattle, sheep and goats with them. Most of these animals died or were sold cheaply to White farmers. In this way African peasants were squeezed off the land and into wage labour.

Well, this time the growing capitalist farmers did not even need the power of guns and cannons to move African people off their land. A growing and brutal system of laws began the process of smashing the independent African peasantry. It was a process which was to continue for many years. The destruction of this class of producers was finally completed only by the 1930s.

We can also see that in the early years of capitalism, the government and the bosses found one of the secrets to profit in the country – a White racist state. This political system went hand in hand with the struggle to control the land and labour in southern Africa.

In Chapter One we have seen how this struggle began with the struggle for land and the growth of trade and agriculture in South Africa.

However, the development of capitalism in South Africa got its biggest boost with the mining of diamonds and gold for profit.

It took the power of monopoly capital in the gold mining industry to organise an effective system of recruiting labour on a large scale. This is the topic of our next chapter.

Chapter Two
Workers on the Mines:
1860s – 1920s

In 1890 there were only 15 000 Africans working on the gold mines. By 1912 there were nearly 190 000 African workers employed on the gold mines.

With the help of the government, the mine bosses were able to recruit this large number of workers cheaply. They developed a cruel system of migrant labour.

African migrant workers actively resisted their conditions. Their struggle was conducted independently of the White working class on the mines.

White workers on the mines formed craft unions to protect their skilled positions. Soon some of these unions allowed semi-skilled White workers to join. These workers now fought for job reservation for White workers to protect their privileged position from the threat of cheaper Black labour.

Militant White workers fought against the bosses and government in South Africa to achieve their aims. In the 1922 strike, they shook the heart of the capitalist system in South Africa.

This chapter discusses these early struggles of workers on the mines.

The chapter has the following parts:

1. **Workers and the Mining Monopolies**

2. **The Cheap African Migrant Labour System**

3. **African Migrants Fight Back – The 1920 Mineworkers' Strike**

4. **Indentured Chinese Mineworkers**

5. **White Workers and Craft Unions**

6. **1913 Mineworkers' Strike**

7. **1922 Mineworkers' Strike**

8. **The Minebosses Fight Back**

1. Workers and the Mining Monopolies

Mining has a long history in southern Africa. Diamonds and gold were not 'discovered' in the late 1800s. In fact, some people had been mining iron from 300 and 400 AD and copper from 700 to 800 AD.

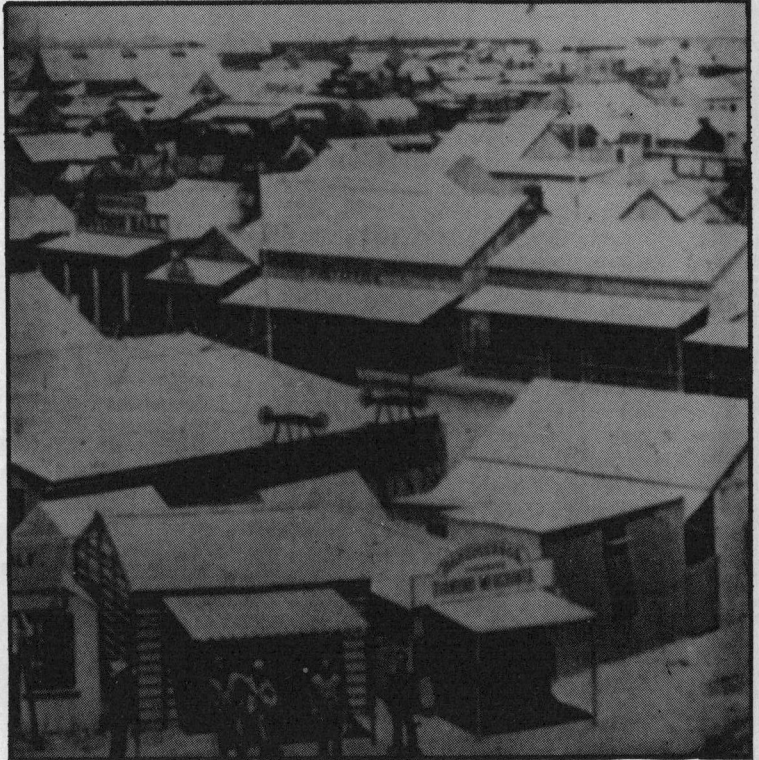

The city of Kimberley grew very quickly after diamonds were mined for profit.

Five years after diamonds started to be mined for profit in Kimberley, five mining companies controlled all diamond diggings in South Africa. These companies became the largest producers of diamonds in the world.

Small, independent diggers were quickly pushed aside by bigger capitalist companies. Mines were owned on a racial basis.

31

This monopoly*, led to the formation of one of the largest and most powerful companies in South Africa called De Beers Consolidated Mines. This company eventually became Anglo-American which today dominates the South African economy. When it was found that large reefs of gold could be mined profitably, the monopoly companies stepped in.

By 1871, there were already 10 000 to 12 000 Europeans and 30 000 Africans working in the diamond diggings. The mining of gold and diamonds for profits greatly increased the need for labour in South Africa.

Because of the shortage of labour in southern Africa, the mine bosses were forced to search for labour from all over southern Africa and even Europe. In 1889, the large mining companies joined together to form the Witwatersrand Chamber of Mines. The Chamber had to find solutions to the common labour problems of the big companies.

Deep level mining* needed workers with different kinds of skills. The mine bosses recruited their workers in at least three different ways:

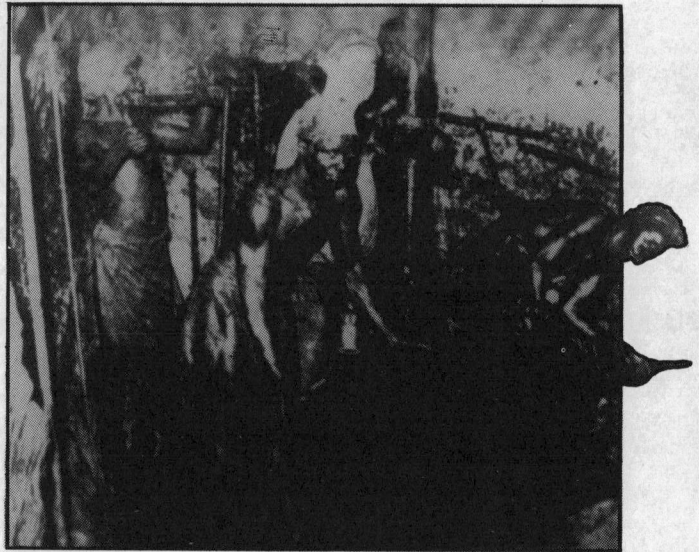

Mineworkers drilling for gold. These workers are standing in water almost two and a half kilometres underground.

- They developed a very large recruiting system to get African workers to work. This system was built around migrant labour.

- Because of the shortage of workers, the bosses were forced to recruit Chinese workers. By 1908 over 100 000 workers had been brought in by the mine bosses under indenture.

- They organised skilled workers to be shipped in from Europe.

These ways of recruiting workers for the mines affected the way that workers organised themselves in the mines. It shaped the way they resisted the bosses and the government.

In the following section we will look at the different ways of recruiting and employing workers. We will also look at the effects they had for worker organisation and resistance on the mines up until the 1920s.

2. The Cheap African Migrant Labour System

By 1912 there were over 190 000 Africans working on the mines.

The mine bosses were able to recruit this number of workers by creating a system of cheap migrant labour*. It was this cheap African labour which became the backbone of the mining economy in South Africa.

Migrant labour did not begin with gold and diamond mining. As early as the 1840s, the Pedi worked as migrants in towns in the East Cape. But it was only after the mining of gold and diamonds for profit that migrant labour was organised on a large-scale.

The laws that were made to control migrant labourers were, in later years, to become a central part of apartheid capitalism* in South Africa.

migrant labour – workers who have to travel long distances to work under contract. They live and work far away from their homes and families for long periods of time.

apartheid capitalism – the political form which capitalism has taken in South Africa, based on strict racial controls placed over the movement of labour.

A recruiting agency finding workers with the help of chiefs.

Recruiting Migrant Workers

The mineowners tried a number ways of getting workers to the mines. From 1889 they tried a system of paying agents to bring African workers to the mines. But this system was not very successful.

It was only in 1896 when the Chamber of Mines formed the Rand Native Labour Association, that largescale efforts were made to recruit workers. Out of this Association grew the Native Recruiting Corporation (NRC) which supplied labour from within South Africa and the Protectorates (Lesotho and Botswana). The Witwatersrand Native Labour Association (WNLA) recruited elsewhere in Africa.

Often the recruiting agency would make an agreement with a chief in an area. The chief would supply a number of workers for the mines. In return he would demand some form of payment, either from the recruiting agency or the workers or both.

The recruiting system did a lot to lessen the labour shortages on the mines. It also stopped competition amongst the mining bosses for labour. Most of the mining companies joined WNLA and all agreed to pay the same low wage to their labourers.

On the mines, the migrant workers lived under very unhealthy conditions in single sex compounds. They slept on cold concrete bunks. The compounds obviously benefited the mineowners in a number of very important ways.

Compounds

- Mineowners paid each worker an 'individual' wage instead of a 'family' wage. They argued that the worker's family still lived from farming in the reserves.

- The compounds were a cheap way of providing accommodation for large numbers of workers.

- The compounds enabled greater production. Workers in the compounds worked more regularly because they could be watched more carefully. They could not leave until they had finished their contracts.

- The compounds were carefully guarded by mine police. This system allowed tight control over worker's everyday lives.

- Workers were often divided into different compounds according to their 'tribe'. This division made resistance difficult.

Mine compound conditions were inhuman.

The WNLA and the compound system alone, were not enough to provide a cheap and sufficient supply of workers for the mines. As time went on, the government was forced to play a far larger part in this recruitment. Especially in the Transvaal, where the mines were very important for the income and survival of the Boer government.

The colonial and Boer governments intervened in three main ways:

1. Passes

In 1896, the Volksraad* in the Transvaal passed two laws. The first law said that all Africans on the Rand must be employed by a 'master' and wear a metal badge on their arm, otherwise they would be put in jail.

The second law divided the gold mining areas into labour districts. When Africans entered a labour district, they had to get a district pass and find work in three days or leave the district.

In 1902, the metal badge was replaced by a signed document giving full details of a worker's history.

2. Taxes

The government imposed taxes to get people to leave their land and go to work on the mines.

- Hut Tax – for every hut owned by Africans.
- Poll Tax – for every man over eighteen years.
- Labour Tax – The Glen Grey Act in the Cape forced Africans to pay ten shillings (R1.00) every year unless they could prove that they had worked for wages for three months.

3. Land dispossession

By the end of the 1800s, most of the land held by Black farmers had been taken over by the government, White farmers and the mining companies. The 1913 Land Act was a major blow to Black landownership.

African workers were coming together from all different parts of southern Africa. But mineworkers did not simply accept the growing system of capitalist oppression and exploitation.

The lives of workers in the mines and compounds were very hard. They had common grievances. By 1920 they were beginning to show that they were willing to fight against their exploitation. In that year, over a period of twelve days more than 70 000 Black mineworkers came out on strike. It was not until 50 years later that a similar number of workers went on strike in the mines!

3. The 1920 Mineworkers' Strike – African Migrants Fight Back

The migrant labour system did not allow for the development of a stable Black working class in one place; a working class which could organise or form trade unions to protect its interests. Strict controls, compounds, mine police and other restrictions made resistance very difficult indeed.

For this reason, resistance was often on an individual basis. Sometimes workers would work until they had enough money to pay their taxes or to buy guns, and then they would desert. They might also desert if wages were too low. Mines where wages were very low and working and living conditions were bad, were often boycotted.

In 1913, soon after the White miners had been on strike, about 9 000 African workers went on strike. This strike against low wages and poor conditions went on for a period of three days.

Some minor improvements were made to workers' conditions after this strike. But it was not enough and African workers went on strike again in 1918 and 1919.

The biggest strike of them all followed in 1920.

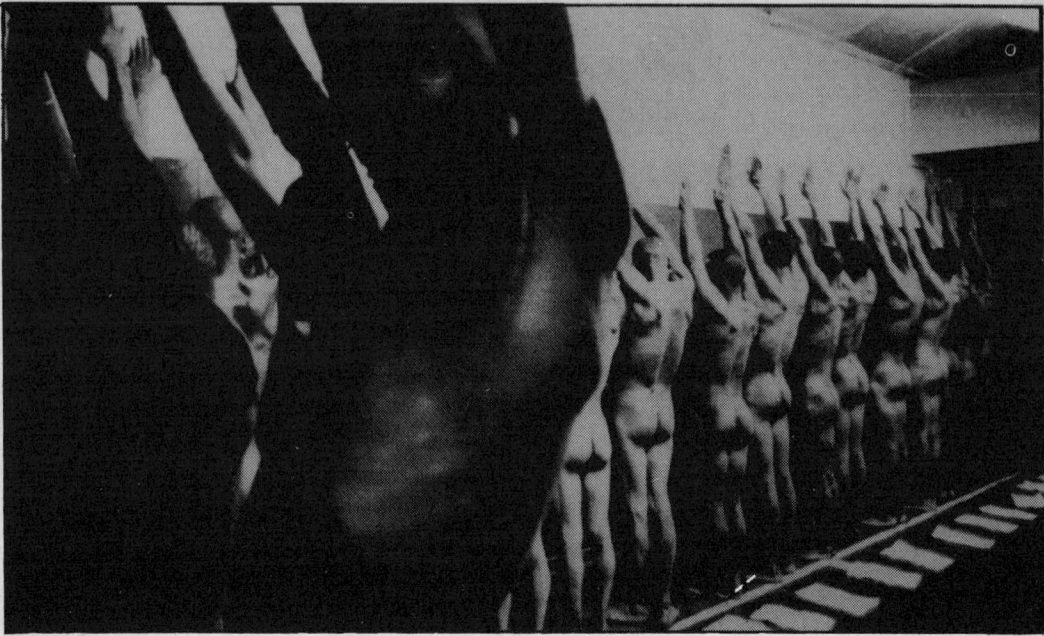

These were the conditions which African mineworkers faced.

This strike began after two mineworkers had been arrested for moving from room to room in a compound, urging workers to strike for higher pay. The day after these workers were arrested, 2 500 workers who lived in the same compound as these workers came out on strike. They demanded that:

- The two arrested leaders were released.
- There should be an increase of three shillings a day in wages. This increase was to keep up with the rising cost of living and to fight hunger and starvation in the reserves.
- Other improvements were made to their living and working conditions.

For six days, over 30 000 mineworkers were out on strike. 21 of the 35 mines were brought to a standstill during the strike. Over 70 000 workers participated in the strike over the twelve days it lasted. The Chamber of Mines said that the strike paralysed the mining industry!

Mineworkers at a meeting in Newtown in the 1920s

But, the mineowners refused to raise the wages of Black miners. The army surrounded the compounds. Workers were beaten and forced underground to work. Workers were arrested, three workers were killed and 40 were left injured.

The strike was a remarkable effort on the part of the growing African working class on the mines.

Hayi! This migrant labour system really helped the bosses. To increase their profits, they got workers from Lesotho, Swaziland, Malawi and especially Mozambique, to come and work on their mines for very low wages.

But this was not enough. By the 1900s they still faced shortages in labour. The mining bosses had learnt from the sugar farmers. They decided to import indentured labour – this time from China!

4. Indentured Chinese Mineworkers

In 1904 the Chamber of Mines Labour Importation Agency was established to get indentured workers from China.

The first 10 000 Chinese workers arrived in the Witwatersrand in May 1904. Chinese workers continued to arrive for the next four years. By 1908, the Chamber of Mines had brought nearly 100 000 Chinese workers to the gold mines.

The Chinese came to work on the gold mines on a three to four year contract. They had to live in the mine compounds while their contracts lasted.

The Chinese miners were not happy with conditions on the mines and some workers left the mines after only a few days.

The Chinese workers did not organise into trade unions, but they had Secret Societies which tried to protect the interests of their members.

In 1905, 1 300 Chinese workers on the North Randfontein mine went on a 'go slow' strike for three days after the manager refused to raise their wages. Fifty-three workers were arrested and charged with public violence.

After 1907, the Transvaal government began to send the Chinese workers back home. They were under pressure from the British government and White miners who were afraid of having their wages undercut

By 1910, the last of the Chinese workers had left the gold mines and were sent back to China.

African and Chinese workers were recruited to do hard and dangerous work on the mines. Their labour increased the mine bosses' profits a lot. But, the bosses could still increase their profits even more. To do this

they needed workers and machines to look for gold very deep down in the earth.

Deep level mining required the use of machinery and skilled workers. To recruit skilled workers for the mines, the bosses turned to Europe.

With their experience of exploitation and organisation against capitalism in Europe, these new workers on the mines were the first to form trade unions in South Africa. But their trade unions were very strange – they protected a certain section of the working class only!

Numbered and finger-printed Chinese labourers pose with compound policemen and supervisors.

5. White Workers and Craft Unions

The first White craft union on the mines was formed on the Witwatersrand in 1892.

The craft unions were able to protect their members through a monopoly of skills. They prevented unskilled White and Black workers from doing skilled jobs.

As the mining industry grew, the mineowners tried to replace some of the skilled White miners with less skilled workers. This was to reduce costs. It became more expensive to mine gold as the mines went deeper underground.

The mine bosses could not raise the price of gold because its price was fixed internationally. So the mineowners had to buy expensive machinery which could speed up production and increase profits. The introduction of new machinery also meant that the mines needed fewer skilled workers to mine diamonds and gold.

Over the years the bosses tried to replace skilled miners with unskilled African miners. This led to many fierce clashes between White miners and the mineowners.

Strikes broke out in 1897, 1902, and 1907 over the reduction of white skilled workers' wages. Less skilled White workers' wages undercut those of the more skilled workers. Strikes also happened because mine bosses tried to reduce the number of skilled workers working on the mines. During the 1907 strike, White workers blew up and wrecked machinery.

During the strikes, the mineowners hired unemployed, unskilled Afrikaners to replace the striking workers at lower rates of pay. 10% of the skilled miners lost their jobs.

To try and protect their jobs, the skilled miners opened their craft unions to unskilled White workers. But they still kept out African workers.

job colour bars – laws which separate workers according to race, into different jobs with different pay rates.

They now united and organised on 'racial' lines. In this way they tried to protect their jobs by limiting the number of people who could do those jobs. They also said those people must be Whites.

The White miners called on the government to protect their jobs from Black workers. Job colour bars* were introduced in 1893, 1911 and 1918 and certain jobs were reserved for White workers only.

Although the White working class organised to protect their own interests, resistance did not end here. Between 1910 and 1922, White mineworkers organised themselves and seriously shook the power of the bosses and the government in South Africa.

White miners on strike in 1913

6. The 1913 Mineworkers' Strike

In 1913, at Kleinfontein mine in Benoni, White workers refused to work the same number of hours on Saturdays as on other days.

The Transvaal Miners' Association and the Transvaal Federation of Trades who represented the White workers on the mines tried to reach a settlement with the mine management. The bosses said that they were not prepared to deal with 'outside' bodies.

The strike spread to all White workers at Kleinfontein and solidarity strikes were organised on other mines. Eventually a successful general strike was called.

The mine bosses agreed to reinstate all workers and look into their grievances. In 1914, the government responded by passing the Riotous Assemblies Act. This law gave the government the power to ban picketing and outdoor meetings. Trade union officials could be charged if any illegal action was taken by the unions.

Soon after the Act was passed, a number of trade union officials were arrested and sent back to England.

But, this was not the end of White worker resistance. They tried everything to protect their jobs. During World War 1 the Chamber of Mines agreed to recognise White trade unions. In 1918 they signed an agreement with the White craft union. This agreement said that for every seventeen Black workers employed on the mines at least two White workers should be employed at skilled rates.

7. The 1922 Mineworkers' Strike

Production on the mines increased between 1914 and 1920. This was a period of stability and profit for the mine bosses. But by 1920 the price of gold was dropping and the bosses were also facing increasing resistance from African workers.

The mine bosses hoped that they could keep down production costs if they lowered the wages of White workers. They also wanted to do away with some of the job colour bars. In this way, they could employ African workers doing the same job but at a lower rate of pay.

At first, the bosses tried to negotiate these issues with the South African Industrial Federation (SAIF). This was a federation of craft unions. But soon the mineowners became impatient with the negotiations.

In December 1921, the mine bosses demanded that the White mine workers' wages be reduced even further. Also, that Whites be removed from a number of semi-skilled jobs, and underground work be reorganised.

The unions refused to accept these changes, and in January 1922 a general strike was called by all White miners. In the following weeks about 25 000 miners went on strike.

At an early stage of the strike, the leadership of the strike passed from the conservative South African

Industrial Federation (SAIF) executive to the militant Council of Action and commandos.

The miners formed local strike committees who elected representatives to a Central Strike Committee in Johannesburg. The Central Strike Committee was established to try and organise and control the strike on the Witwatersrand.

Workers also organised themselves into commandos. The commandos tried to stop scab workers from entering the mines and they attacked African workers who tried to go to work. The slogan of a number of White miners was, 'Workers of the World Unite and Fight for a White South Africa'.

The strike lasted for eight weeks and was followed by two weeks of armed revolt. Some commandos held secret meetings and planned to overthrow the government. They attacked police stations so that they could get more guns.

The government responded with bullets and bombs. They sent 7 000 heavily armed troops and a number of bomber planes to deal with the strikers. Over 500 people were injured, and 153 people were killed in the clashes between the army and the commandos. 5 000 strikers were arrested and imprisoned or had to pay fines. Four men were sentenced to death and hung as a result of the strike.

By March 1922, the mines were operating again. The White mineworkers' strike had been crushed! This allowed the mineowners to make changes on the mines which were necessary to increase their profits.

8. The Minebosses Fight Back

After the defeat of the workers, the mine bosses were able to make a number of changes on the mines. They reduced White wage rates by between 25% and 50%. They also withdrew two paid holidays.

The agreement of 1918 was scrapped, the recognition of shaft and shop stewards withdrawn, some colour bar regulations were dropped and the whole industrial relations system was destroyed.

In its place the government passed the Industrial Conciliation Act of 1924 which recognised White trade unions and included them in a bureaucratic system to solve workers' grievances, while curbing the militancy of White workers.

The mine bosses also reorganised work on the mines. Many Whites lost their jobs to African workers who were paid much lower wages. Blacks took over semi-skilled manual work such as drill-sharpening, waste-packing, engine-driving, pumping and carpentry.

On the other hand, many White miners became supervisors. The mine bosses did not place any Africans in supervisory positions and this entrenched the racial divisions amongst workers on the mines.

Chapter Three
Building Capitalism!
Manufacturing:
1920s – 1940s

During the 1930s and through the 1940s, the capitalist economy in South Africa grew very quickly. This was especially in the manufacturing sector* of the economy. By 1943, the manufacturing sector had overtaken gold and agriculture as the largest sector of the economy, and the biggest employer of workers.

manufacturing sector – industries which need machinery to make new products in factories.

These developments had a major impact on worker organisations. Hundreds of thousands of workers now joined trade unions.

craft unions – unions for workers who have special knowledge of how to make something. The power of workers in these unions is this knowledge or skill.

Craft unions* for skilled workers were forced to change their constitutions to allow semi-skilled workers to join. The first White industrial trade unions were formed.

The number of African workers increased rapidly. New machinery on the mines, and the growth of larger factories gave African workers greater bargaining powers. For the first time African workers began to form industrial unions.

But why did South African capitalism grow so quickly during these years?

This chapter looks at some of the reasons why capitalism grew so quickly in these years.

It also looks at the strict controls placed on the working class in these years.

The chapter has the following short sections:

1. **Protecting South African Manufacturers**

2. **The Parastatals**

3. **The Price and Production of Gold**

4. **Government Laws – Dividing and Controlling the Working Class**

5. **Machines and Semi-skilled Workers**

1. Protecting South African Manufacturers

During World War 1 between 1914 and 1917, international trade was seriously disrupted. This gave a small class of South African manufacturers*, the chance to start making some goods which were usually imported from overseas. They could do this without overseas competition.

manufacturers – capitalists who own factories and machinery where goods are made to be sold.

But after the war, capitalism expanded and South African manufacturers had to find some way of protecting themselves from the cheaper goods manufactured in Europe and imported into the country. To do this the bosses and the government followed a policy known as 'industrial protectionism'*.

industrial protectionism – laws which make it expensive for capitalists from other countries to sell goods in a particular country. These laws protected the profits of the capitalists in this country.

This meant that South African industries were protected from competition with overseas capitalists. Tariffs* were imposed on a number of goods entering the country.

tariffs – money which has to be paid when goods are imported into a country.

- The Board of Trade and Industries was established in 1921, which advised the government on ways of assisting and developing industry in South Africa.

- The Pact government* passed the Customs Tariff and Excise Duty Amendment Act which gave further protection to South African manufacturers.

Pact Government – an alliance between the Labour Party and the Nationalist Party which came to power in 1924.

These laws helped South African manufacturers, but they could only invest their money in industries which did not need large amounts of capital.

If capitalism was to expand, the country needed a transport system, steel and electricity and other basic infrastructure*. Here the government was willing to lend a hand.

infrastructure – things like roads, railways, electricity and water supply.

49

An ISCOR plant rolling the first cast of metal blocks in 1934. The ready local supply of metal enabled South African heavy industry to develop very rapidly after 1945.

parastatals – companies which are established and owned by the government.

2. The Parastatals*

- In 1910 the government established the South African Transport Services (SATS) to co-ordinate transport around the country.

- In the 1920s and 1930s the government spent large amounts of money on irrigation for capitalist agriculture.

- In 1922, the government set up the Electricity Supply Commission (ESCOM). ESCOM went a long way to providing the country's electricity needs.

- In 1928, the government also established the Iron and Steel Corporation (ISCOR) at a cost of R7 million.

- In 1940 the government announced that there would be further expansion of ISCOR and established the Industrial Development Corporation (IDC) to provide finance for industrial expansion.

Industrial protection and government financed industry provided important support for South African capitalism. But this would never have happened if not for the gold mining industry.

3. The Price and Production of Gold

Between 1931 and 1940 the price of gold increased by 98% and the value of South Africa's gold sales increased by 155% – from R92 million to R236 million.

In these years new machinery was bought and production speeded up. Many new mines were also opened and profits came rolling in.

Excess Profits Tax – a high tax placed on profits on the mines.

The government taxed the profits made by the mines. In the mid-1930s the Excess Profits Tax* was passed, and between 1933 and 1939, one-third of all government money came from gold mine taxes.

Government protection, parastatals, and gold were all very important to the growth of capitalism. But on their own this was not enough.

The real key to the success of capitalism from the 1920s through to the 1940s lay elsewhere – this was in the way that the government was able to help provide the bosses with a cheap and strictly controlled working class.

4. Government Laws – Dividing and Controlling the Working Class

The mineworkers were crushed in the strike of 1922. This weakened White working class organisation. The government was now able to pass a number of laws which entrenched divisions in the working class, and killed the militancy of White workers.

51

- **1924:** The Industrial Conciliation Act – aimed to divide workers, including trade unions for skilled workers. This law restricted workers from striking. A complex industrial relations system tried to stop worker militancy.

- **1925:** The Wage Act – established a Wage Board. The Wage Board was meant to fix wages for semi-skilled work. At the time many White workers had semi-skilled jobs. The Board had to maintain a 'civilized' rate of pay for unskilled White workers.

- **1926:** The Job Reservation Act and the Mines and Works Act – these laws firmly entrenched the colour bar in industry and certain job categories were protected for Whites.

These laws were very important in maintaining and controlling a cheap and divided workforce. But the major way that the bosses and the government tried to control and supply workers was by strict controls over the African working class, and a final attack on the already diminishing peasantry.

The rapid expansion in the economy caused some problems for the bosses as their labour needs underwent great changes. Once again, the bosses began to be faced with labour shortages.

By the end of the 1930s, 93 000 of the 236 000 workers in the manufacturing industry were Whites. The bosses and government now turned to Black labour to increase the supply of workers, and to keep labour costs down.

Enough cheap labour had to be provided in all the major sectors of the economy – mining, agriculture and manufacturing – in a way that would not affect the supply to any one branch of industry.

In the 1930s, the government passed a number of laws to control the supply of Black labour. These laws reorganised the supply of workers in three main ways:

- The number of Africans who were allowed to work was increased.

- The places where they could work was strictly controlled.

- When Africans did find work in urban areas, they were strongly disciplined and strictly controlled.

In the 1930s the bosses and the government spent no money on workers' houses – Cato Manor shantytown.

A number of laws were passed to do this:

- **The Native Urban Areas Act of 1923**
  This law controlled the movement of Africans and restricted the movement of Africans once they were living in the cities. It denied Africans political rights and restricted their rights to own land in the cities.

- **Amendments to the Immigrations Act**
  Amendments to the Immigration Act between 1931 and 1937 allowed the mining bosses to recruit workers from countries north of South Africa.

- **The Hertzog Bills of 1936**
  These laws increased the farmers' control over labour tenants, curbed squatting and prevented the flow of Africans to urban areas. The laws also further limited African and Coloured political rights.

- **The Native Land and Trust Act**
  This act was one of the final legal attacks on the peasantry and placed more restrictions on the right of peasants to own land.

- **The Native Laws Amendment Act of 1937**
  This law restricted the number of Africans entering the cities by only allowing Africans to stay in the urban areas if they had a job.

Government controls over African workers helped the bosses secure their labour needs at very low rates of pay. Between 1933 and 1939 an additional 240 000 Africans were employed in manufacturing. Between 1940 and 1946, this figure increased by 115 000.

In these years there were major changes in both the numbers and composition of the South African working class. The growth of factories, and new machinery also changed the kind of work which workers were doing. This had a large effect on the way they could organise into trade unions.

5. Machines and Semi-skilled Workers

consumer product factories – factories which make goods for personal use.

Until 1930, manufacturing had been dominated by small consumer product factories.* But between 1930 and 1955 there were important changes in the type of goods which were being produced.

Metal products, machinery and transport industries became the largest industrial groupings within manufacturing.

mass production – the large-scale and fast production of goods with the help of machines.

The growth of the metal, and machine industries was heavily dependent on the mass production* of goods. These industries needed semi-skilled machine operators.

The bosses used new methods for organising workers in the factory to speed up production and increase profits. These new methods were called scientific management. Scientific management separates the planning of production from doing the job.

This is what the Board of Trade and Industries said about scientific management:

'The planning of production is separated from doing the job. The planning people look at the whole job that has to be done (for example, a car has to be made). They decide what is the best way to do it. The workers will do the different parts of the job as they are told to do.'

54

Industrial apprentices in the early 1930s

With scientific management and the use of machinery, production did not need a lot of different skills. It needed many workers with similar skills. To keep profits up, production also needed people to control and supervise the workers in the factory.

The new machinery was a threat to the jobs of skilled workers at first. But the skilled White workers increasingly became supervisors during the 1930s. This strengthened the existing racial divisions on the shopfloor.

So, in the 1920s a process began which continued right through to the 1970s. The work of skilled workers was increasingly handed over to semi-skilled African workers at lower rates of pay. On the other hand, skilled workers moved into supervisory positions with much higher wages.

However, these new conditions did have some advantages for worker organisation.

Between 1915 and 1930 the number of people employed in private industry doubled from 101 178 to 201 180. This increased the power of the working class and their ability to resist the government and the bosses.

55

To keep costs to a minimum, manufacturing capitalists began to draw workers from three sectors of the population:

- Large numbers of people under the age of 21 were employed. This was because these workers were not entitled to the full rate of pay.

- White women were employed. In 1935 the Industrial Legislation Commission* said that women should receive two-thirds of the pay given to men.

Industrial Legislation Commission – a commission (group of people) set up to look at the laws for industries and factories.

- African men were employed at low levels of pay. At this time African men had very little protection from the law.

The Industrial Conciliation Act of 1924 forced workers to organise along industrial lines. In terms of the act, agreements were negotiated for the industry as a whole.

Wage determinations by the Wage Board were meant to stand for all workers, irrespective of race. Although African workers were not recognised by law as 'employees', they could for the first time, bring their grievances to the attention of the authorities by making representations to the Wage Board.

Once a wage determination had been made, African trade unions could organise to try and make sure that bosses were paying the full rates of pay.

Strict controls over the movement of workers, changing methods of production, laws to divide the working class, no recognition of African trade unions, strong government support for capitalists – these were the conditions under which South African capitalism grew in the 1930s and 1940s.

These were also the conditions under which workers were forced to organise.

African workers moved into more skilled jobs but still received low wages.

Chapter Four
The First Industrial Unions:
1920s – 1930s

The growth of the manufacturing economy gave a big boost to the development of trade unions in South Africa.

Large numbers of semi-skilled workers now entered the factories. These workers could not organise and defend themselves around their skills like the workers from craft unions did earlier. They realised that their power came from their numbers. Trade unions began to organise all workers, regardless of their skills.

Many craft unions began to include semi-skilled workers in their trades, and registered industrial unions were also formed.

But in the 1920s, the trade union movement was seriously divided. Although there was some non-racial worker solidarity, African workers could not officially join registered trade unions as they were not recognised as 'employees' in the 1924 Industrial Conciliation Act.

In 1919 Africans formed a general union, the Industrial and Commercial Workers Union (ICU) to defend their interests. But, by the late 1920s, African workers had also begun to organise their own industrial trade unions.

These African trade unions came together in their own federation.

This chapter discusses these developments in the 1920s and is divided into the following sections:

1. **Craft Unions and the South African Industrial Federation**

2. **The First Industrial Unions: The South African Trade Union Council – 1925 to 1930**

3. **Non-racial Worker Action in the 1920s**

4. **The International Socialist League (ISL) and the First African Trade Unions – 1915 to 1920**

5. **The Industrial and Commercial Workers Union (ICU) – 1919 to 1930**

6. **The South African Federation of Non-European Trade Unions (FNETU) – 1928 to 1932**

1. Craft Unions and the South African Industrial Federation

Craft unions were not only formed on the gold mines. In the late 1800s a number of craft unions were formed in industries which serviced the mines.

At first, in the 1880s and 1890s, a number of British craft unions opened branches in Durban, Kimberley and Johannesburg. Printing workers from the Transvaal, Cape Colony, Rhodesia and Natal came together to form the South African Typographical Union. This was the first South African craft union which did not start as a branch of a British union.

The craft unions organised skilled workers only and tried to prevent unskilled Black and White workers from doing their jobs at lower rates of pay. In the 1880s and 1890s, these craft unions went on strike for higher pay and shorter working hours.

Trades and Labour Councils – organisations which were the first attempts at uniting craft unions.

By the 1900s, Trades and Labour Councils* were formed in the big towns to try and unite the different craft unions. These councils also tried to get Labour candidates* voted onto the town councils.

Labour candidates – people from the Labour Party who stood in the election for parliament.

The Trades and Labour Councils in the different provinces were replaced by Industrial Federations which dealt only with trade union work. The different Industrial Federations came together to form the South African Industrial Federation (SAIF).

The SAIF was active in the Rand Revolt of 1922, but after this strike trade union membership fell dramatically from close to 110 000 to 80 000. The SAIF collapsed.

First meeting of SATUC – 1925

2. The First Industrial Unions: the South African Trade Union Council – 1925 to 1930

The large number of workers moving into manufacturing were far more militant than the skilled workers. Their wages were low, and conditions poor. To oppose the power of the bosses they had to organise as many workers as possible. Unlike the skilled workers, they could not rely on on their skills alone to protect their continued employment.

These workers built trade unions which organised all workers regardless of their skills. At the same time, some craft unions were forced to open their unions to all workers regardless of their skills, because of the increasing use of machinery in the factories.

After the SAIF collapsed in 1925, the Minister of Labour, Colonel Creswell, called a special congress of trade union representatives to form a trade union co-ordinating body. The Minister of Labour wanted to be able to negotiate with a single body representing all trade unions. He hoped that in this way industrial legislation could be more smoothly implemented.

The Communist Party of South Africa (CPSA) was formed in 1921, and changed its name to the South African Communist Party (SACP) in 1953.

At this meeting, the South African Trade Union Council (SATUC) was formed. Bill Andrews, a member of the South African Communist Party (SACP)*, was elected as secretary at the first congress of SATUC. His election came as a surprise to the organisers of the congress.

From the start, SATUC showed the growing influence of the more militant new industrial unions. Many of the older craft unions such as the South African Typographical Union (SATU) and the Mineworkers Union (MWU) refused to join SATUC and this gave the newer unions far more power.

Women who had recently moved into low paid jobs in the manufacturing industry played a leading role in trade union organisation during this time. 75% of the members of the militant Garment Workers Union (GWU) were women.

The GWU grew from a craft union – the Witwatersrand Tailors Association (WTA). To protect the interests of its members, this union was forced to open its doors to less skilled workers. Many of these workers were women.

In August 1926 the constitution of the union was changed to allow Indians and Coloureds to join. By 1930, the membership of the union grew to 900 and the GWU gave support to the African Clothing Workers Union.

Between 1928 and 1932 the union led over 100 strikes, two of which brought the whole clothing industry to a standstill!

The increase in the number of women being employed led to attempts to form a Women Workers Union (WWU). Fanny Klennerman attended the 1925 Annual Conference of SATUC on behalf of the newly formed Women Workers Union (WWU) and demanded that SATUC support the WWU.

distributive trades – refers to shop or retail workers.

The WWU helped women workers in the distributive* trades, and consistently fought for womens' interests in the male-dominated SATUC. The union was responsible for organising the Sweetmakers Union. A Waitresses Union was also formed, but it did not last very long.

Although SATUC organised mainly White workers, it was important for the support and assistance it gave to the organisation of new industrial unions in the 1920s.

Some of these unions included:

- Furniture Workers Union – formed in 1925 and had 800 members by 1930
- Sweetmakers Union – formed in 1925
- Boot and Shoemakers Union – formed in 1926
- Reef Native Trade Assistants Union – formed in 1926
- Canvas and Rope Workers Union – formed in 1927
- Transvaal Leather Workers Union – formed in 1929.

3. Non-racial Worker Action in the 1920s

The growth of manufacturing industry brought Indian, Coloured, African and White workers together in the workplace as semi-skilled workers.

These workers were often doing very similar jobs under the same conditions. Divisions amongst workers along racial lines had not yet been entrenched. At this time, activists and trade unionists believed that there was a very real chance for non-racial class action in the manufacturing industry. Workers also showed this solidarity through united action.

Genuine solidarity was most clearly shown in the garment, leather, furniture and canvas unions. In these industries the colour bar against Indians and Coloureds doing certain kinds of work was dropped.

parallel unions – these unions were formed alongside registered trade unions. They usually organised only African workers who were not registered under industrial legislation. These parallel unions were subordinated to the registered union and helped control African workers rather than advance their struggle.

- Both the Garment Workers Union and the Furniture Workers Union held joint meetings with parallel* African unions in the same industries.

- The Johannesburg Boot and Shoe Workers Union accepted Whites, Coloureds and Africans as members of the union.

- The registered unions and African unions in the laundry industry had a joint executive committee.

- In 1928, 400 White workers went on strike at the Germiston clothing factories to resist victimisation. The Native Clothing Workers Union in the factory also came out in support. The dismissed workers were reinstated.

defence pact – an agreement which attempted to bring closer unity between unions.

- In 1929 the unregistered African union in the furniture industry signed a defence pact* with the Furniture Workers Union.

SATUC was strongest on the Witwatersrand and did not have much support outside of the Transvaal. But in other parts of South Africa, workers were active in building industrial trade unions.

In Natal, the Natal Indian Congress (NIC)* helped build Indian trade unions. Most of the White unions did not accept Indian workers. Some NIC members argued that Indian workers should form unions and use the Industrial Conciliation Act of 1924 to win better wages and working conditions.

Natal Indian Congress – a political organisation which was formed by Mahatma Gandhi in the late 1800s to represent the political aspirations of Indian people in South Africa.

In 1928, the NIC helped form the Natal Workers Congress (NWC). The NWC was also known as the Indian Trade Union Congress and included trade unions from the liquor and catering, bakers, tobacco, and laundry industries.

The NWC did not last for long, although some of the individual unions did continue to function. The unions grew weaker during the depression of 1929 and 1933. But Indian workers gained some experience of trade unionism and they began to reorganise during the late 1930s.

In the Cape, racially mixed unions had been in existence before the formation of SATUC. Many of these unions had joined together in the Cape Federation of Labour Unions (CFLU).

At first the CFLU distanced themselves from the SATUC, which had only White members, as they believed that it was a racist organisation.

But by 1928, SATUC recognised that its member unions were in favour of organising all workers in a particular industry in one union. Even the right-wing unions recognised that Black workers should be organised even if this was to be in a parallel structure.

In the 1920s, African workers began to organise trade unions for the first time. These trade unions were organised independently of the structures of registered trade unions.

In 1919 African workers formed a general union, the Industrial and Commercial Workers Union (ICU). When this union was at its strongest, it claimed a membership of 100 000. But by the late 1920s African workers also began to see the advantages of organising industrial trade unions.

4. The International Socialist League and the First African Trade Unions – 1915 to 1920

A poster of the ISL showing the unity of White and Black workers.

In 1915, the International Socialist League (ISL) was formed by some members who withdrew from the White South African Labour Party (SALP)*. It was the ISL which first began to try and organise African workers.

South African Labour Party – a political party formed to promote the interests of White workers.

In Durban in 1917, the ISL helped form the Indian Workers Industrial Union. They also helped to form unions in the printing, tobacco and hotel industries. They also organised dock workers, but this did not last for very long.

The ISL was active on the Witwatersrand as well. In 1917 they helped form the Industrial Workers of Africa (IWA) on the Rand. In 1918, striking municipal workers on the Rand were assisted by the IWA.

In June and July of 1918, the IWA launched a one-shilling-a-day campaign. They called on employers to raise workers' wages to a minimum of one shilling per day and threatened to call a general strike if the bosses failed to do this.

The police responded quickly. They arrested members of the ISL and IWA, smashing attempts to organise the general strike.

The ISL was also active in Cape Town. But these two organisations, the ISL and the IWA, did not last for very long. They also did not really ever grow very big. But they did have some influence among African workers, especially on the Witwatersrand. They helped workers during the 1920 African mineworkers' strike.

But it was only with the formation of the Industrial and Commercial Workers Union (ICU) in 1919, that African workers began to organise on a mass scale throughout South Africa.

The South African Communist Party

In July 1921, the Communist Party of South Africa was formed (renamed the SACP in 1953). This party was formed by members of the ISL and other small left-wing groupings.

At first the SACP was mainly a White organisation. Members believed that inter-racial working class solidarity would grow with the development of White worker consciousness.

The party was active in the 1922 Rand Revolt. In 1924, the party began to change its policy. The SACP said, 'Our main revolutionary task was among the natives.'

In 1928, the SACP adopted a policy that said that party activists should work towards 'an independent native republic as a stage towards a workers' and peasants' republic.'

The people who supported this idea said that because some people in South Africa were oppressed as a nation, socialism would have to be reached by two phases.

national democratic
revolution – a revolution
which tries to unite all
people across all classes in
one country. The revolution
ensures that all people have
a say in the election of the
government of that country.

The first part of the struggle was for a national democratic revolution*. This meant that different classes would unite to fight the issues that oppressed them.

So the SACP demanded co-operation from different organisations until a national democratic revolution had been achieved. After this, the struggle for socialism could continue.

The policy of trying to include Africans in their organisation had a major effect on the way in which the SACP viewed trade unions.

The party established a relationship with the ICU. But, the Communists were eventually expelled. Many members of the SACP were also involved in organising African industrial trade unions in the 1920s right through until the 1950s.

First meeting of the CPSA – 1921

INDUSTRIAL & COMMERCIAL WORKERS UNION OF AFRICA.

Established January, 1919.

Branches throughout the Union of South Africa and South-West Protectorate.

All Correspondence to be addressed to the General Secretary.

HEAD OFFICE
24 LOOP STREET, CAPE TOWN.

PHONE NO. 5320 CENTRAL.
TELEGRAPHIC ADDRESS : ".ISEEYOU" CAPE TOWN.

Official Organ : "THE WORKERS HERALD."

5. The ICU – 1919 to 1930

In 1912, the South African Native National Congress (later the African National Congress – ANC) was formed to protest against the proposed passing of the Land Act. The organisation was made up largely of members of the African middle class and tribal chiefs.

In the 1920s it was the Industrial and Commercial Workers Union (ICU) which far surpassed the ANC in militancy and mass support. At times this led to disagreements between the two organisations.

The ICU was first formed by African and Coloured dock workers in Cape Town in 1919 and soon started organising workers in other industries. It became a General Union* organising workers in the docks, textile, food, clothing, engineering and agricultural industries.

general union – this kind of union organises workers from all industries into one union.

The union grew very quickly and by the mid-1920s had branches in Port Elizabeth, East London, the Central and Eastern Cape, the Orange Free State, the Transvaal and Natal.

In 1919 and 1920 the ICU was active when dock workers in Port Elizabeth and Cape Town went on strike for higher wages. In Port Elizabeth the police opened fire, killing 21 people and injuring many more.

By the late 1920s, the ICU leadership, especially secretary Clements Kadalie, tried to steer the union away from strikes and militant action. This led to conflict amongst the leadership.

Some people in the ICU started calling for direct action in the form of strikes, the burning of passes and a refusal to pay taxes. These radicals – most of whom were members of the Communist Party – were not happy with Kadalie's tactics. They were also critical of the way in which the finances of the ICU were being handled.

Disagreements arose between Kadalie and the members of the Communist Party. In 1926, Communist Party members were expelled from the ICU. Workers in a number of branches of the ICU protested against these expulsions.

Kadalie began to concentrate on getting the support of White liberals, and on negotiating with the government.

When strikes broke out in Durban, Northen Natal and the Transvaal, the ICU refused to offer the striking workers assistance. At times they encouraged workers to return to work rather than strike.

By 1927, the ICU claimed to have 100 000 members. But, there were no clear structures to represent workers in the ICU. The officials in the ICU had a lot of power and were directly involved in making policy decisions.

By 1928, the membership began to fall. After expelling the communists, the ICU spent very little time organising industrial workers. They did get support from labour tenants who thought that they may get their land back if they joined the ICU. The ICU spent a lot of time and money on court cases against White farmers on behalf of farm workers.

Well, we can see clearly that there were problems with the structure of the ICU. These problems in the way ICU was organised, were some of the reasons why it got a lot weaker in the 1930s.

Even while the membership was growing in the Transvaal, members in the Cape began to leave the ICU. By the early 1930s, the ICU had split into a number of different sections and soon collapsed.

The Decline of the ICU

There were many fights within the leadership of the ICU.

In 1928, Kadalie tried to expel AWG Champion, the secretary of the Natal branch of the ICU. Champion, with the support of Natal members of the ICU, broke away from the main organisation to form the independent ICU *yase Natal* with about 30 000 members.

Durban system – a system where the Durban municipality had a monopoly over the brewing and selling of beer. The profits made from this were used to administer the control of the African townships.

In Natal, the ICU took up the beer struggle and the 'Durban system'* was fiercely resisted by many Africans around Durban.

The Beer Hall Riots in Durban, and the Anti-People Dipping Campaign* were highpoints in the ICU's struggles in Natal.

A group of branches in the northern Orange Free State also broke away from the union.

Anti-People Dipping Campaign – at this time Africans from rural areas were dipped like cattle before they were allowed into the cities.

In 1928, trade unions in Britain sent a trade unionist called Ballinger to assist the ICU. But Kadalie and other ICU officials did not get on well with Ballinger.

After a quarrel with Ballinger, Kadalie left the ICU and set up the Independent ICU in 1929. By this time the ICU had lost many of its members and neither the ICU under the leadership of Ballinger, nor Kadalie's Independent ICU lasted long after this.

The ICU also had to face the power of the government and Whites in general. By the late 1920s, they were trying to crush the ICU. Legislation was used to restrict the movement and activities of ICU activists. ICU offices were raided and union furniture and documents burnt.

*Cato Manor women face batons as they protest **against** the 'Durban system'.*

So, what happened to the ICU? There were some good things and some bad things.

By the end of the 1920s officials in the ICU were accused of stealing money and the organisation had almost disappeared.

Although the ICU failed to build a strong democratic organisation for workers, it was a major advance for the struggle of African workers against exploitation and oppression.

The ICU:

- Helped to overcome tribal divisions by bringing workers from all over the country into one organisation.

- It provided workers with some experience of trade unionism which they could build on.

- The ICU made the rest of the world aware of the bad conditions under which the Black working class had to labour.

But even while the ICU was still alive, workers had begun organising in different trade unions. These were not general unions like the ICU, but industrial unions. In 1928 they had formed the first federation of industrial unions for African workers in the history of the South African working class.

6. The South African Federation of Non-European Trade Unions – 1928 to 1932

Formation of the FNETU

The first African industrial unions began to appear early in 1927. This was largely due to the work of Communist Party members who supported the 'Black republic' slogan.

After some Communist Party members were expelled from the ICU in 1927, they began to organise the urban industrial working class which the ICU left behind.

In March 1928, 150 delegates representing 10 000 workers from different African industrial trade unions, came together and formed the South African Federation of Non-European Trade Unions (FNETU).

The FNETU followed a different strategy to the ICU. FNETU saw itself strictly as an industrial trade union body which would deal with working conditions, demand a 48 hour week and equal pay for equal work.

The shortage of labour and the growth of manufacturing increased the power of African unions in the late 1920s. In 1927, over 4 000 Blacks went on strike as opposed to 740 Whites. In 1928, 5 000 Africans went on strike while only 710 Whites were involved in strike action.

These strikes were usually either in response to the victimisation of trade unionists, or to force payment of the legal wage rates laid down by the Wage Board.

The FNETU and many of its member unions had a very hard time during the depression of the early 1930s.

Worker activity amongst Africans increased in the late 1920s. But of all the African unions formed between 1927 and 1929, only the South African Clothing Workers Union, and the African Laundry Workers Union lasted through the depression.

Decline of the FNETU

Despite this increase in worker activity amongst Africans in the late 1920s, the FNETU and many of its member unions crumbled during the depression of the early 1930s. Most trade unions collapsed during the depression because:

- African trade unions were still not recognised by law.

- The depression weakened the bargaining position of workers.

- This situation was made worse by the general climate of repression during this time. The police had large powers to interfere in the affairs of trade unions.

- Manufacturing was not well developed and consisted of a number of small capitalists employing a few workers in each factory. This made organisation difficult and meant that the trade unions could not mobilise large numbers of workers.

- Squabbles within the Communist Party spilt over into the trade unions and in 1930 many members who had trade union experience were expelled from the party.

With few worker controlled structures built into the practice of the trade unions and no concrete gains being made for these workers, the unions simply dissolved.

But workers had gained experience from joining trade unions, and during the 1930s the long and painstaking effort to build industrial unions continued. Right through to the 1950s, the majority of African workers belonged to a separate trade union federation from the larger registered trade unions.

We will discuss these developments in the next two chapters.

Chapter Five
The South African Trades and Labour Council: 1930s – 1950s

In 1930 representatives of the Cape Federation of Labour Unions (CFLU) and the South African Trade Union Council (SATUC) came together to form the South African Trades and Labour Council (SATLC).

Between 1930 and 1955, the SATLC was the largest body of trade unions in South Africa.

In the early 1930s, the older craft unions were able to dominate the more militant trade unions in the SATLC. By the late 1930s and 1940s, things began to change. Both industrial unions and the African working class, had grown in size and power. They seriously challenged the control of the craft unions.

Very few African workers joined the trade unions affiliated to the SATLC, but the relation of African workers to the SATLC played a large part in leading to the eventual collapse of the Council.

This chapter discusses the struggles of the trade unions which were affiliated to the SATLC.

The chapter is divided into the following sections:

1. **Affiliates of the SATLC**

2. **Industrial Unions and the Workers' Charter**

3. **The Break up of the SATLC**

1. Affiliates of the SATLC

At its inaugural conference, the SATLC called for the full recognition of African trade unions and the abolition of all discriminatory legislation.

But the SATLC was not a tight federation of trade unions with a uniform policy. Within the affiliates of the SATLC there were very different levels of democracy and political policy.

As a result, some of the affiliates of the SATLC gave assistance to African workers and their trade unions. But many of the trade unions were openly racist.

Within the SATLC there were four major groupings of trade unions. These were:

- Conservative craft unions
- White racist industrial trade unions who often relied on the government for support
- Racially mixed industrial trade unions which organised Black workers as junior partners in their unions
- Non-racial industrial trade unions which organised all workers within the limits placed upon them by the bosses and the government

We see that these unions often followed very different strategies. These differences were very important as they caused the eventual collapse of the SATLC. Let us look at each grouping in turn.

Craft Unions

During the 1930s and 1940s, the craft unions tried to protect their members whose skills were being replaced by machines. Many craft unions were forced to open their doors to less skilled members. This was often not to protect the semi-skilled workers, but to give the skilled workers greater control over all decisions affecting workers in the factory.

For example, the Amalgamated Engineering Union (AME), which had 7 608 members in 1947, slowly allowed semi-skilled workers to enter their union. Other craft unions were not as willing to follow this strategy.

The Iron Moulders Society (IMS) – a small union with 501 members in 1937 and 1 182 ten years later – would not include workers in their union unless they had completed their apprenticeship.

operative labour – workers who operate machines.

Eventually in 1947 the IMS agreed to allow semi-skilled operative labour* to perform many more tasks in the industry.

closed shop – an agreement which says that only the majority union is allowed to represent workers in a factory or company. The factory is closed to other unions.

To keep a closed shop*, White semi-skilled workers were allowed to join the IMS. The union protected these workers by strictly defining the work of their semi-skilled members. Non-union African labour was then barred from doing this work.

The union did give in to some reclassification to allow Africans to do some work at cheaper rates of pay. But this was always in return for further guarantees and privileges for the registered union.

White workers working on an assembly line in a motor car plant, where mass production divided jobs into smaller tasks and speeded up production.

At this time, semi-skilled White workers tried to protect their jobs in different ways. The older craft unions in the SATLC tried to protect semi-skilled workers by strictly defining jobs. Other White workers formed industrial unions which were openly racist. These unions were formed by semi-skilled White workers in industries where their jobs were threatened by cheaper Black labour.

White Industrial Unions

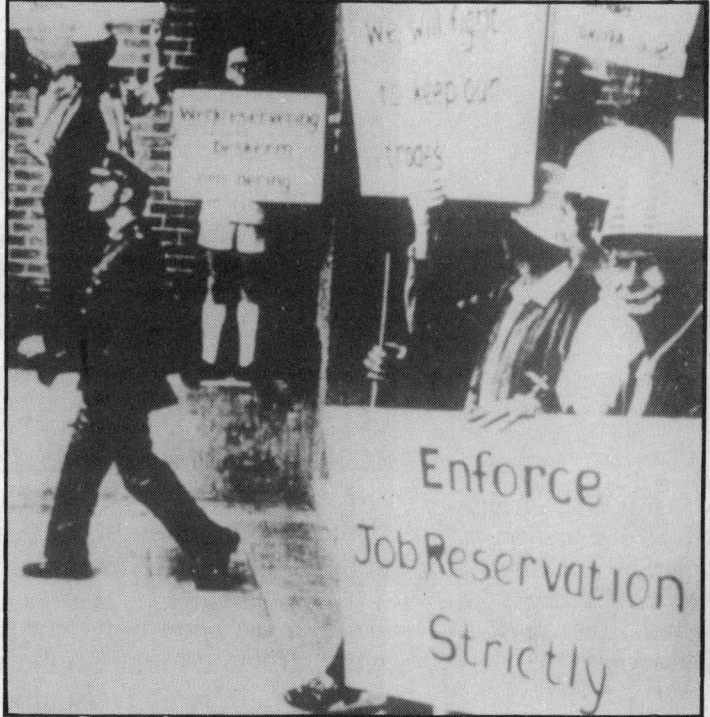

White workers fight to keep their jobs through job reservation.

The White racist unions used all the weapons they could to make gains for their members. They turned to the government and their membership for support.

This form of trade unionism was most successful in industries where White workers relied directly on the government for their employment. But the White industrial unions were not united in their response. Some of these unions were closely tied to Afrikaner

Nationalism. They were united with other White industrial unions through their common racism.

In the 1930s, the ideas of Afrikaner nationalism began to spread. At first, these ideas were supported by the Afrikaans speaking middle class in the larger towns. They then turned to the Afrikaans workers and unemployed for support.

But many workers did not agree with Afrikaner nationalism. It only had small pockets of support in industries where White workers depended directly on the government for employment and protection.

Afrikaner nationalists were anti-imperialist and anti-communist and denied that there was any conflict between capitalists and workers. They supported racial separation as a way of protecting White workers from competition from Black labour.

Afrikaner Nationalism had support within the White Mineworkers Union (MWU) as well as from White workers on the railways.

Afrikaner Broederbond – a secret organisation, formed in the 1930s to protect and promote the interests of middle class Afrikaners.

In 1934 the Spoorbond was formed on the railways by the Afrikaner Broederbond*. The Spoorbond had some success amongst the Afrikaans workers who relied on the government for their jobs.

Neither the Spoorbond nor the Mineworkers Union were affiliated to the SATLC. But this did not mean that there were no racist unions in the SATLC. Some industrial unions, such as the South African Iron and Steel Trades Association (ISTA), were openly racist in their organisation.

The South African Iron and Steel Trades Association (ISTA) was established in 1936 with a membership of 300 workers. Since this time it has grown to become one of the largest White unions. In 1976 it had a membership of over 38 000. It has played a major role in organising the right wing of the trade union movement.

In ISTA, White workers were mobilised as workers in

an industrial union. The majority of membership was drawn from the White semi-skilled operatives.

ISTA was openly racist and proposed a policy of White leadership for racially mixed unions.

In 1947 ISTA led a breakaway of five Pretoria based trade unions from the SATLC, after a motion to expel African trade unions had been defeated. The Co-ordinating Council of South African Trade Unions (CCSATU) was established in 1948 and was dominated by ISTA. The CCSATU would not accept affiliation from any trade union in which Blacks held voting rights.

The CCSATU was the first grouping of trade unions to break away from the SATLC. It broke away because it supported racist policies.

Not all the trade unions within the SATLC were openly racist. Some unions tried to organise all races in some way. But this did not mean that all members in the union were equally represented.

'Parallelism'* and Mixed Industrial Unions

parallelism – a name used to describe trade unions which are organised by race, separate from registered unions.

By the 1930s and 1940s, Whites who had led militant action in the 1920s, were moved into higher paying supervisory and clerical jobs. Black workers now moved onto the factory floor. These White workers still remained members of industrial unions, but slowly began to represent a privileged group within the factory.

The Furniture Workers Industrial Union (FWIU) and the Garment Workers Union (GWU), both affiliates of the SATLC, were examples of such unions.

Furniture Workers Industrial Union

During the 1920s, the craft unions in the furniture industry in the Transvaal opened its doors to Indian and Coloured workers and helped to form an African union in the industry.

81

But the bureaucracy of the FWIU feared that African workers may undercut their members' wages. They refused to allow African workers to join the union as equal partners.

The FWIU used the industrial council and bargaining rights in the factory to maintain privileges for their members.

The African Furniture, Mattress and Bedding Workers Union (FMBWU) often complained about the demands made by the FWIU at the industrial council. The FWIU refused to support a motion calling for the inclusion of the FMBWU on the industrial council.

By the 1930s and 1940s, the bosses began to employ cheaper Black labour in the garment industry. The GWU tried to protect the interests of its large White membership.

It tried to control the demands of Black workers by including them in parallel structures of the union which had less power than White workers.

PLEASE STAY AWAY FROM MACHINE AND DON'T ANNOY WORKERS!

BROEDERBOND

GARMENT WORKERS UNION

Garment Workers Union

In 1935 the GWU established a Number 2 Branch of the union for Coloured members. They were not allowed representation on the executive of the GWU.

By 1942, the executive of the Number 2 Branch pushed for direct representation on the executive of the union and the industrial council. This demand was rejected by the leadership of the union.

The Number 2 Branch was expelled in 1944 and were only readmitted after a half-hearted vote of confidence in the leadership of the GWU.

Parallelism was imposed on the Coloured membership by the executive. Africans were also organised in a separate body and made up another level of parallelism.

In both the FWIU and the GWU, Black workers were not given equal representation with White members. As junior partners in the union, Black workers were unable to make an impact on the trade unions.

Unions like the FWIU and the GWU eventually joined the Trade Union Council for South Africa (TUCSA) in the 1950s. TUCSA continued to organise African workers into parallel unions right up until the 1980s.

Other unions within the SATLC were firmly committed to the principle of non-racialism.

Non-racial Registered Trade Unions

The Food and Canning Workers Union (FCWU), the Textile Workers Industrial Union (TWIU), and the National Union of Laundry, Cleaning and Dyeing Workers (NULCDW), followed a different strategy to those in the furniture and clothing industries.

These three unions operated in industries where there
had been a large drop in the number of Whites
employed during World War 2. Most jobs involved
semi-skilled workers and racial divisions were difficult
to implement.

The Food and Canning Workers Union and the African Food and Canning Workers Union

In the food and canning industry, African and
Coloured workers were doing similar jobs. This made
it important for workers to organise non-racially.

Even when the FCWU was forced by law in 1947 to
separate racially, the registered union maintained very
close relations with the African FCWU. It affiliated to
the non-racial South African Congress of Trade
Unions (SACTU) in the 1950s.

*A canning factory organised by the Food and Canning Workers
Union*

Textile workers belonging to the TWIU picketing during a strike in 1935.

The Textile Workers Industrial Union

In the 1940s, expansion in the textile industry was achieved mainly with the employment of African male workers in semi-skilled and unskilled positions. Wages were low for Black and White workers. In 1935 when Whites were still doing productive work*, attempts were made to organise African workers.

productive work – in this case, productive work means that the majority of Whites were supervisors.

The Cape Town and Harrismith branches of the union were completely non-racial. The TWIU also insisted that African workers should be represented on the industrial council.

As with the FCWU, when a separate branch of the union was formed for African workers in the 1950s, a close working relationship was maintained between the different branches.

These four groupings of trade unions came together in the SATLC:

- craft unions
- White industrial unions
- mixed industrial unions
- non-racial industrial unions.

In the early years of the SATLC, the craft unions were able to dominate the Council. But by the late 1940s, industrial unions had grown in power and strength. They managed to gain control of the SATLC.

INDUSTRIAL AND 'CRAFT' UNIONS IN THE SATLC 1931 – 1947

Year	'Craft' Unions	Industrial Unions
1931	7	16
1937	7 7 871 members	25 8 809 members
1947	15 70 855 members	79 60 033 members

MAY DAY 1938

2. Industrial Unions and the Workers' Charter

The National Executive Committee of the SATLC was elected on a block card vote system. This meant that each affiliated union had one vote which counted for their whole membership. This system favoured the larger craft unions who were able to dominate the SATLC. In 1938, the industrial unions were able to gain control of the NEC by amending the constitution to allow the NEC to be elected by industrial groupings.

From this time the SATLC adopted a more militant position. Local committees were established. These committees had no clear relationship to the NEC. But a number of the militant activists in the trade unions argued that the Local Committees could provide the basis for non-racial working class solidarity.

At times they did. For example, some Local Committees supported the 1946 African mineworkers' strike. This was despite the fact that the SATLC had argued that police action during the strike was necessary. But the Local Committees also faced many problems and were often dominated by the craft unions.

The most public statement of the politics of the SATLC was the Workers' Charter of 1944.

The Workers' Charter recognised the need for socialism. It was a major advance in formulating the political and economic demands of the working class.

In 1943 a Workers' Charter committee was elected. This committee broke into sub-committees to deal with different parts of the Charter.

The Charter was a victory for the more progressive forces in the SATLC. A 'National Charter Campaign' was launched to 'mobilize the trade union movement' to have the Charter made law.

Extract from the Preamble of the 1944 Workers' Charter

'The people of South Africa are not prepared to go back to the conditions of the pre-war world, nor will they accept the uncertain and unplanned anarchy of production and distribution visualised by the most reactionary sections of the capitalist class.

The organised workers in the trade union movement know full well that the only solution to our problems lies in South Africa adopting Socialism as our form of government, which will bring emancipation to the working people from exploitation and oppression and will place the common people in control of South Africa. This must be the aim of the trade union movement.

But we cannot sit back with folded arms to await the "Socialist Dawn", nor does it mean that we cannot in the course of our struggle win great improvements for the workers of South Africa, despite resistance which is being and will be exercised by the capitalist forces to maintain their privileged position. That is why we put forward our Workers' Charter, embodying fundamental demands that the trade union movement believes can be brought to fruition for a post-war South Africa, where security of employment, freedom from want and poverty, with a happy and prosperous life, can be attained for all our people irrespective of race, colour, creed or sex.'

The Workers' Charter was accepted at a special conference of the SATLC in 1944. But it did very little to change the conservatism of the affiliates of the SATLC.

In 1947, the SATLC had an affiliated membership of 184 041. By 1954 this membership had become deeply divided. The uneasy alliance could not last forever.

---

3. The Break up of the SATLC

In 1947, the first unions broke away from the SATLC. They protested against African unions being allowed to affiliate to the SATLC. They then formed the Co-ordinating Council of South African Trade Unions (CCSATU).

The CCSATU represented seven unions with a total membership of 13 000.

A far larger split occured in 1950. Craft unions, together with other White and mixed industrial unions, representing 100 000 members, broke away and formed the South African Federation of Trade Unions (SAFTU).

In 1950 a split emerged over the passing of the Suppression of Communism Act. Some unions argued that the SATLC should mobilise its members against the passing of the bill.

The craft unions, together with conservative mixed and White industrial unions supported the bill. They eventually left the SATLC to form the South African Federation of Trade Unions (SAFTU).

These unions were more interested in protecting their members against the threat of cheaper African labour than in building non-racial unity.

By 1952 the SATLC had been severely weakened. Its only affiliates were industrial unions. It adopted a resolution condemning the Suppression of Communism Act and tried to mobilise support nationally and internationally to defend those banned under the Act.

SA TRADE UNION CO-ORDINATING BODIES IN 1954

Co-ordinating Body	Membership	Comments
SATLC	80 000	semi-skilled industrial unions; 5 African unions and the rest 'mixed' (Indians, Coloured, Whites) unions
SAFTU	100 000	craft, mining and municipal unions, Transvaal furniture workers; White or 'mixed' unions
CCSATU	13 000	iron and steel workers and local Pretoria unions; White unions
WPLU	17 000	local unions; mostly 'mixed' unions
SAR&H Staff Associations	70 000	White railway unions
CNETU	10 000	unregistered African unions
Unaffiliated	122 000	

Throughout its history, only six African unions were ever affiliated to the SATLC at any one time and by the mid-1950s, those industrial trade unions remaining in the SATLC were deeply divided over the issue of African trade unionism.

Some argued that a strict policy of non-racialism should be followed. This would make an alliance with the old craft unions impossible.

Others argued that the non-racial industrial unions should follow the softer line of parallelism. In this way they could maintain an alliance with the craft unions and increase their bargaining power.

At a May Day demonstration in Cape Town 1937, workers demanded 'No Colour Bar in the trade unions'.

The SATLC was caught in a trap. Either they had to forget the craft unions and join the African trade unions. Or they could try and call the craft unions back. If they joined the African trade unions, they would lose a lot of power. If they called the craft unions back, they would have to compromise on racial issues.

In 1954, the executive chose the second path and laid the basis for the re-establishment of an alliance with the craft unions at the expense of African workers.

A Unity Committee was set up by leading members of the SATLC, SAFTU, Western Province Federation of Labour Union (WPFLU) and the Amalgamated Engineering Union (AEU). African trade unions were excluded from the conference discussions.

Out of these discussions, the South African Trade Union Council (SATUC – later TUCSA) was formed.

In 1954 the SATLC dissolved, but only half of its membership joined SATUC. SAFTU, on the other hand, did not dissolve. Half of its membership (mainly the craft unions) affiliated to SATUC.

Most of the African and non-racial trade unions in the SATLC opposed the proposals made by SATUC. The NUDW, TWIU and the FCWU were barred from joining SATUC. These unions, except for the NUDW, joined with the CNETU unions to form the South African Congress of Trade Unions (SACTU) in 1955.

It was SACTU which took up the struggle for non-racial industrial unions through the remainder of the 1950s and into the 1960s.

So far, we have only discussed what was happening in the largest trade union federation between 1920 and the 1950s. The story for most African workers was very different. They had very few bargaining rights and were excluded from industrial relations machinery. For African trade unions, the period 1930 to 1950 was a struggle for survival!

Chapter Six
The Struggle to Survive:
African Trade Unions:
1930s – 1940s

After the collapse of the FNETU, the next major attempt to organise a federation of African trade unions was the formation of the Council for Non-European Trade Unions (CNETU), in 1941.

The CNETU was formed after ten years of struggle. African trade unions that were crushed during the depression, had to be rebuilt.

During World War II, the membership of CNETU grew very fast. By 1945, the CNETU claimed an affiliated membership of 158 000 workers in 119 trade unions. This accounted for about 40% of all Africans working in manufacturing and commerce.

The 1940s were a highpoint in trade union resistance, yet by 1950 the CNETU had been severely weakened.

This chapter discusses these struggles of African trade unions in the 1940s.

The chapter has the following sections:

1. **African Trade Unions in the 1930s – The Limits to Wage Bargaining**

2. **The Formation of the Council for Non-European Trade Unions (CNETU)**

3. **Workers and War – The Right to Strike**

4. **The 1946 African Mineworkers' Strike**

5. **The Politics of the CNETU**

6. **The Decline of the CNETU**

7. **African and Indian Industrial Trade Unions in Durban**

1. African Trade Unions in the 1930s – The Limits to Wage Bargaining

industrial councils and wage boards – organisations which set minimum wages for different industries. At this time some industries had industrial councils where the bosses negotiated minimum wages for the whole industry, with the registered trade unions. In other industries, the minimum wage was fixed by the Wage Board.

Trade unions were weakened by the collapse of the FNETU. So in the 1930s, many trade unionists used the small bargaining spaces available for African workers, such as industrial councils and wage boards*.

In this way some gains were made for workers. However, this strategy had a number of limits for building democracy and mobilising workers around issues which affected them in their everyday lives.

Wage Boards and Industrial Councils

The passing of the Industrial Conciliation Act in 1937 was a major advance in the rights of African workers. The Act excluded African workers from industrial councils. Instead, the Act said that African workers should be represented by an official from the Department of Labour.

The Minister of Labour refused to accept an industrial council agreement unless it had fixed wages for African workers. For the first time, the wages of Black workers in the building, engineering and steel industries were regulated.

In the late 1920s, the Wage Board was one of the most liberal of all the government bodies. In 1928 and 1929 it fixed wages for the baking, laundering, furniture and clothing industries.

The African General Workers Union (AFGWU) was formed for workers employed in industries controlled by industrial councils. The registered unions on the industrial councils made it very difficult for African workers to organise. Trade unions for Africans were more successful in those industries where no strong registered trade unions existed.

In industries where there were no industrial councils, minimum wages were laid down by the Wage Board.

Trade unions in these industries presented evidence at public sittings on wage boards.

It was only after workers saw that they could get concessions from the wage boards and industrial councils, that they began joining trade unions in large numbers. The trade unions spent their time trying to ensure that concessions and minimum wages set down by the industrial councils and wage boards were implemented.

Unions were formed in over twenty industries, but there were clear limits to this organising strategy.

The unions concentrated on presenting evidence at a national level to government bodies around wage issues. They did not mobilise workers around shopfloor issues.

So workers had very few other ways to push their demands. If presenting cases to the wage boards and industrial councils failed, then no gains could be made. As a result worker organisation in the factory was not very strong.

During the war years, African workers were in a stronger position. This was because the bosses and the government needed to maintain production to make sure that the war effort was not disrupted.

This demand for labour gave workers more confidence. There was an increase in strike action and African trade unions began to grow in numbers, size and militancy.

2. The Formation of the Council for Non-European Trade Unions

By 1939, 20 000 workers from eleven different unions worked inside a joint committee. This body was known as the Joint Committee of African Trade Unions (JCATU).

Another grouping of African trade unions also developed in the early 1940s. These were centered around the African Clothing Workers Union (ACWU). Gana Makabeni, the secretary of the union, received his wages from the Number 1 Branch of the Garment Workers Union (GWU). In 1940 Makabeni was elected secretary of the Co-ordinating Committee of African Trade Unions (CCATU).

In November 1941 the JCATU and the CCATU met on the Witwatersrand to take steps to federate under a Council for Non-European Trade Unions (CNETU).

Twenty-five trade unions represented at the meeting, claimed a membership of 37 000 workers.

The real strength of the CNETU was on the Witwatersrand. By 1945, it claimed to have 119 affiliated trade unions representing a membership of 158 000 workers.

CNETU MEMBERSHIP IN 1945

Centre	No. of Unions	Membership
Johannesburg	50	80 000
Pretoria	–	15 000
Bloemfontein	10	5 000
Kimberley	5	3 000
East London	10	15 000
Port Elizabeth	19	30 000
Cape Town	10	10 000
Total	119	158 000

The African working class grew more militant during the war years. We can see this in the rapid growth of the CNETU. African workers were in a stronger position because of the demand for labour to keep production going during the war. But as the war progressed, stricter controls were placed on African workers by the government and the bosses.

3. Workers and War – The Right to Strike

To meet the demands of the war, the government and the bosses needed industrial peace and stability. The government was granted greater powers to deal with any situation which they felt might hamper the war effort, and in 1942 they passed War Measure No. 145.

This law made all strikes illegal. It took away one of the most important weapons in workers' struggle against the bosses and the government. But, some workers ignored the law. They continued to strike.

A strike broke out in the coal yards on the Witwatersrand in June 1944. 1 000 coal workers walked out from their jobs and refused to deliver coal except to hospitals and charitable institutions. The strike ended in a victory for the workers. In a new wage agreement, workers received higher wages, overtime pay and shorter working hours.

The coal strike was a great victory. But this did not mean that the bosses and the government were prepared to recognise workers' right to strike. They used strong-arm tactics to divide workers and break strikes.

Workers came out on strike throughout 1943 and 1944 in defiance of anti-strike legislation. But most of these actions ended in defeat. One of the worst defeats suffered was at the Victoria Falls Power Station.

The power station supplied the mines with electricity. The African Gas and Power Workers Union (AGPWU) made a claim to the Wage Board for wage increases. Workers were told that they would have to wait until a report had been submitted by a commission of inquiry into the mining industry.

When the delay lasted for a number of months, about 2 300 workers came out on strike. The strike was crushed by calling in Coloured soldiers to keep the machines running, and the workers' compounds were surrounded by police and army troops. Workers were interrogated and a number of the 'ring leaders' sent back to the reserves.

The war time raised many debates amongst workers. There were different ideas about what action to take.

Workers could only strike illegally. This tactic left them open to police attacks. But workers showed that they were still willing to take this risk in their fight against the bosses and the government.

Their differences came out into the open during the milling workers' strike in 1944.

1944 – Members of the Milling Workers Union

The Milling Workers' Strike

Many of the leaders of the CNETU were members of the South African Communist Party (SACP), or the African National Congress (ANC), or both. In 1945, Gana Makabeni was replaced as president of the CNETU by JB Marks – chairperson of the African Mineworkers Union, member of the Communist Party and the African National Congress.

During the war, the major White and Black political organisations, including the ANC and the All Africa

Convention (AAC), many African chiefs, and the leadership of the CNETU, supported the South African government's war effort.

They called on workers not to strike and believed that countries should unite to defeat Hitler, the fascist dictator of Germany, who was a threat to world peace.

The SACP argued that Germany should be defeated because of its threat to the Soviet Union. They felt that the Soviet Union should be defended.

As a result, the SACP appeared to hold a similar position to other organisations that supported the war effort.

But for the SACP, strikes were to be a last resort. Within the CNETU there was some opposition to this position.

A group of trade unionists and political activists argued that the war was not so much a matter of defeating Hitler. Rather, it was a way in which capitalists could make bigger profits by investing in arms and machinery. This group said that the war was an imperialist war and could not be defended on any grounds. However they did believe that the USSR should be defended from attack.

On 24 May 1944, unions in the milling industry made demands for increases in wages and a reduction in the number of working hours. This demand came after the wage agreement in their industry ended. The Department of Labour told the union that its case could not be heard, as the Milling Workers Union was not recognised under the Industrial Conciliation Act of 1924.

arbitrator – a third person who comes in to look at the problem and tries to settle it.

On 11 September the union called for an arbitrator*. after it received no reply, 2 000 workers came out on strike for ten days.

The bosses met worker representatives on the first day of the strike, but then failed to reply to requests. After that, they entered into no further negotiations. Scabs were brought into the mills.

Workers who tried to form picket lines were arrested. The police fined seventeen workers for public violence and imposed restrictions on two union officials. During the strike, 600 workers were arrested for holding a public meeting of more than twenty people.

To prevent the Milling Workers Union (MWU) from coming under police attack, the strike was co-ordinated by a group made up of various union officials. This body became known as the 'General Staff'.

The milling workers' strike was resolved and 70% of the workers were reinstated immediately. The rest were reinstated over three weeks. But, the 'General Staff' did not dissolve.

The 'General Staff' stated that the milling workers' strike had shown the weakness of the CNETU, and that the trade union movement was in a bad way. They argued that the only way in which the government could be stopped from implementing anti-worker and anti-trade union policies was through a general strike.

The milling workers' strike had been resolved successfully. This had been the first major test for the CNETU. The second came when 60 000 mineworkers went on strike after a call by the African Mineworkers Union (AMWU) – an affiliate of the CNETU. The CNETU then called for a general strike in support of the mineworkers.

4. The 1946 African Mineworkers' Strike

The African Mineworkers Union

In 1941, the Transvaal section of the ANC called a conference to discuss the formation of a mineworkers' union. The conference was attended by 80 delegates from 41 different organisations.

The meeting elected a committee of fifteen to raise funds and help build a union in the mines. The union would organise workers in the mines and in the reserves before they went to work in the mines.

JB Marks, a member of the ANC and the CPSA, was elected president of the African Mineworkers Union (AMWU). The vice-president was James Majoro, a member of the Native Mine Clerks Association (NMCA) which eventually affiliated to the African Mineworkers Union.

From the start, the compounds were closed to the AMWU and the union had to rely on individual contacts between the Native Mine Clerks Association and workers underground.

Despite these problems there were a number of work stoppages throughout the early 1940s. Five years later, the union had grown to 25 000!

Work stoppage in 1944

At its annual conference in August 1944, the AMWU discussed the findings of the Lansdown Commission. This commission had been set up by the government to look into the conditions and wages of mineworkers.

Although the report was rejected by the conference, the executive of the AMWU discouraged strike action because of the war effort. The executive said that the findings should be implemented as a step in the right direction. They demanded a Wage Board inquiry into the industry, and for other unions to protest against mineworkers' conditions.

But, this was not enough. Workers continued to protest against their conditions. At the 1946 annual conference of the AMWU, 2 000 delegates drew up a list of demands to present to the mining bosses.

The African Mineworkers Union demanded:

- a minimum daily wage of ten shillings
- family housing
- two weeks paid leave every year
- 100 pounds gratuity after fifteen years of service
- payment of repatriation fees*
- the repeal of War Measure 145 which had hindered the organisation of workers on the mines, by prohibiting meetings of over twenty people on mining property.

repatriation fees – money that the Lesotho government took from the workers who were going to work in South Africa.

A number of attempts were made by the union to negotiate these proposals with the Chamber of Mines, but they were ignored.

The Miners' Strike

In August 1946, about 1 000 delegates at an open air meeting of the AMWU called for a strike. They also warned that violence should be avoided.

Workers went on strike on Monday 12 August. By Saturday 17 August, the miners were forced to return to work.

Police were brutal in their attack. 1 600 police were placed on special duty. The compounds were sealed off under armed guard. At least twelve workers were killed and over 1 200 injured. Leaders of the strike committee were arrested.

The police played a big role in crushing the 1946 mineworkers' strike.

After the strike, the Chamber of Mines released a statement claiming that 76 000 workers, out of a total workforce of 308 000, had stopped work.

Two months before the strike, the CNETU had resolved to support the mineworkers if they went on strike. They called for a general strike of Black workers. But workers were cut off from their leaders and lived under armed guard in the compounds. They also received very little support came from other unions.

Eventually the CNETU was forced to drop the call for a general strike.

The defeat of the mineworkers seriously weakened the CNETU. Only 36 unions were represented at the 1947 conference. Of these, only six had paid affiliation fees, and eight were not affiliated to the council at all.

At this conference the CNETU was also seriously divided. Divisions which had emerged in the milling workers' strike were never resolved. The 'General Staff', which had developed during the strike, did not dissolve but, was transformed into the Progressive Group of Trade Unions (PTU) which worked within the CNETU.

There were serious differences between the PTU group and the CNETU leadership.

5. The Politics of the CNETU

By 1944 the CNETU had become a Transvaal Council for Non-European Trade Unions (TCNETU), after an agreement had been reached with twelve African trade unions in Pretoria.

Mike Muller, a full-time organiser for the SACP, was the general secretary for the Pretoria unions. There was one secretary for every two of these twelve unions. These secretaries were either members of the CPSA or sympathised with the Communist Party's position.

By 1945, the leadership of the CNETU was dominated by the SACP.

The PTU group set itself up as a caucus* within the CNETU and called for the dismissal of the leadership.

The PTU group argued that:

- The 'salvation of the workers lies in a strong powerful council'. The number of strikes that were occurring in South Africa showed that the working class was unhappy with their conditions and dissatisfied with the policies followed by their leaders.

- They were anti-war and saw no need to support Smuts' South African government. They wished rather to concentrate on winning political and economic rights for workers.

- They demanded that African trade unions be recognised. Unlike the CNETU leadership who argued that African workers should be included under the provisions of the 1924 IC Act, the PTU group called for the unconditional recognition of trade unions.

- The PTU group called for a minimum wage of three pounds per week – as opposed to the CNETU's demand for two pounds per week – and for a sliding scale of wages*.

- The PTU group wanted the CNETU to launch a massive drive to include unorganised workers in unions and to campaign for these demands.

These issues were debated at two conferences which CNETU called in 1945 to discuss trade union matters. At these conferences the PTU group, were attacked for being 'adventurists' and a 'danger and menace to the Africans'.

The major debate at the second conference revolved around the need to form a national co-ordinating body for African trade unions.

The PTU group was in favour of a strong national central body. The body's task was to launch a massive organisational drive to revive the existing unions, and to bring more workers into industrial unions.

caucus – here this means a group of people who meet within an organisation to discuss and organise around their political position.

sliding scale of wages – wages automatically tied to increases in prices and the cost of living.

The SACP was split over the issue. Some members from Cape Town believed that African unions should affiliate to the SATLC. Members from the Transvaal, together with the PTU group, were in favour of an independent national council for African trade unions.

No resolution was passed at the conference and the matter was referred back to the CNETU.

The PTU group were unhappy about this decision and did not believe that anything would come of it. They organised a number of 'call-back' meetings to mobilise and inform workers about the position. Although four meetings were planned, only two took place.

The larger of these two meetings was at Market Square in Johannesburg and drew a crowd of 7 000 workers who were informed of the decisions taken at the conference.

Soon after this meeting the CNETU expelled two leaders of the PTU group – Phoffu and Koza. They said that Koza and Phoffu had made a false statement about Gana Makabeni and the misappropriation of funds. They also said Phoffu and Koza had held a factional meeting at Market Square.

By 1950 the CNETU had been severely weakened by divisions as well as the crushing of the mineworkers' strike. Centred mainly on the Witwatersrand, its membership had dropped from 158 000 in 1945 to 17 296 in 1950.

6. The Decline of the CNETU

After two officials were expelled from the CNETU, the PTU group formed the Council of African Trade Unions. They complained of a lack of consultation and attacked the CNETU's relationship with the SACP and ANC.

Although this new council attracted 22 unions it soon collapsed, and most of the more solid African unions remained with the CNETU and played an important role in the formation of the South African Congress of Trade Unions (SACTU) in 1954.

The CNETU was strong in the Transvaal, but had little impact on trade unions in Natal. During the 1930s and 1940s, Indian and African workers in Natal formed industrial trade unions which were either affiliated to the SATLC, or independent of any national body.

This experience of trade union organisation helped lay the basis for workers in Natal to join other trade unions under SACTU in the 1950s.

7. African and Indian Industrial Unions in Durban

Between 1930 and 1950 there were 85 strikes in Natal, involving nearly 16 000 Black workers. Most of the strikes took place in Durban, in the food, beverages and tobacco industries. These strikes involved both Indian and African workers. They showed the need to build non-racial trade unions in Natal.

The most important of these strikes took place at the Falkirk iron and steel company in 1937. In 1942 there was also a major strike at Dunlop Rubber.

The bosses broke the strikes by dividing workers. Migrant African workers were used to replace striking Indian workers. The bosses also built their 'own' company unions to try and destroy non-racial trade unions.

The Durban District Branch of the Communist Party was very active in helping to build non-racial trade unions.

Some unions were formed on racial lines and had only Indian or African membership. The Communist Party also helped to form parallel African unions of registered industrial unions.

By 1950, most of the trade unions that had been formed in Durban in the 1930s and 1940s had collapsed. Many trade unionists were prevented from doing work before and after the Suppression of Communism Act was passed in 1950.

A few unions like the Durban Indian Municipal Employees Union (DIMES) and the National Baking Industry Employees Union (Natal) survived, but they were taken over by a moderate leadership.

These unions, together with the conservative unions like the Garment Workers Union and Furniture Workers Industrial Union joined TUCSA in the 1950s. In 1947, African workers formed the Natal Federation of African Trade Unions (NFATU). Five unions affiliated, but the federation had collapsed by 1948.

Trade union members march through the streets of Durban.

Despite this trade union collapse, the experience of trade unionism in these years laid the foundations for the rapid growth of non-racial trade unionism in Durban in the late 1950s and early 1960s.

Chapter Seven
Apartheid Regime on the Attack: The 1950s

The 1950s were a period of great upheaval and of repression and resistance, in South Africa.

Although there had been economic expansion in the country during World War 2, profits on the gold mines had fallen. The 1950s were also a time when the manufacturing industry did not expand. The reserves could no longer support the people who lived there. The whole cheap labour system was being seriously threatened.

However, the apartheid regime through its massive racist and bureaucratic control over workers, backed up by a strong police force, managed to save the cheap labour system.

At the same time it effectively divided the working class organised in trade unions.

This chapter discusses these events and is divided into the following sections:

1. **The Economy – Increasing the Supply of Labour**

2. **The Nationalist Party Comes to Power**

3. **Trade Union Politics in the 1950s**

1. The Economy – Increasing the Supply of Labour

By the 1950s the growth of the economy, increased the needs of the mining, manufacturing and farming bosses for cheap labour. This was for slightly different reasons.

Gold Mining Industry

Profits in the gold mining industry fell during World War 2. But in the 1950s profits on the gold mines expanded very rapidly.

During the 1950s, the mining bosses increased the supply of labour to the mines by recruiting more workers from outside South Africa. They also raised capital to buy more machinery to speed up production on the mines.

Between 1946 and 1960, the size of the Black working class on the mines increased by 30%. Over 60% of these workers were recruited from outside South Africa.

Manufacturing Industry

GDP – Gross Domestic Product – this is the total money value of all the goods produced within a certain country.

By the 1940s, manufacturing was contributing the largest share to the GDP*, but the manufacturing economy was dominated by a number of small industrial companies. For example, between 1953 and 1954, 65% of all industrial companies employed less than nine workers per company.

industrial output – the quantity of goods produced in industry.

By the 1950s, manufacturing capitalists were facing competition from overseas capitalists. The rate of increase of industrial output* was falling.

The Growth of Industrial Output	
1954	7,2%
1955	44%
1956	3,4%
1957	2,3%
1958	1,7%
1959	minus 1,4%

To expand their industries, these capitalists could no longer afford to invest large amounts of capital in new machinery. They hoped to increase productivity through increasing the number of workers in the factories.

Agriculture

The collapse of the reserves provided major problems for the agricultural bosses. In the reserves families could no longer support themselves. People were moving to the cities to look for work. This threatened the supply of workers to the farmers.

The farming bosses had to make sure that enough workers remained in the countryside to serve their labour needs and to keep wages as low as possible.

Apartheid agriculture: Sowing the seeds of worker militancy.

We can see that during the 1950s, workers would have to be heavily controlled, if the bosses still wanted to maintain and expand their profits. This control would ensure a cheap supply to all these sectors.

Once again, the government came to their rescue. This time it was the Nationalist Party which came to power in 1948.

2. The Nationalist Party Comes to Power

After the Second World War, the Nationalist Party (NP) appealed to White voters over two major issues.

- It promised to solve the labour crisis in the country.
- It promised to smash the political threat presented by Black trade unions and other organisations.

The NP government passed laws which weakened the position of the working class, entrenched migrant labour, and limited the rights of all Blacks in urban areas.

These laws affected all areas of workers' lives:

- **no Black landowners in White farming areas**

influx control – control over the movement of workers coming from the bantustans into the towns.

In the 1950s, influx control* was tightened and more strictly enforced. There was a campaign to stop Blacks owning land in White areas, and African squatting and labour tenancy* on White farms was prohibited.

labour tenancy – farm workers are rented a piece of land as part of their wages for working on the farm.

- **resettling Africans**

In 1951, the Prevention of Illegal Squatting Act allowed the Minister of Native Affairs to force Africans to move from any land to resettlement camps.

- **labour bureaus**

The Native Laws Amendment Act of 1952 set up a system of labour bureaus. Africans could not leave a rural district until all the labour requirements in that district had been met. This meant that labour could be controlled and distributed to those areas where it was most needed.

- **reference books**

In 1952, the Natives (Abolition of Passes and Co-ordination of Documents) Act stated that all Africans had to carry 'reference books' and that African women were to be included in the influx control system.

- **building townships**

In 1951, the Native Building Workers' Act said that Africans were not allowed to do skilled building work unless they were working in African townships. They would also be paid one third less than other workers who do similar work.

- **Bantu Education**

The Bantu Education Act passed in 1953 set up a separate educational system for Africans under the control of the Department of Native Affairs.

- **attacks on the oppressed**

The Group Areas Act of 1950, allowed the Minister of the Interior to set aside land for the occupation or ownership of different 'races'. This law was used to move thousands of people into African townships.

The Separate Representation of Voters Bill in 1951 removed Coloured voters from the common voters' roll.

- **police repression**

Besides these laws, the government and the bosses also used the full force of the police to back them up. The Suppression of Communism Act of 1950, the Public Safety Act and the Criminal Law Amendment Act gave the police and government a great deal of power to interfere in any action which they might see as a threat to their position.

These laws affected workers and the oppressed. The NP government also passed laws which dealt with the way workers were allowed to organise themselves on the factory floor.

- **no recognition for African trade unions**

  In 1953, the government passed the Native Labour (Settlement of Disputes) Act which set up a separate industrial relations system for African workers.

  African trade unions were not prohibited, but they had no access to the industrial council. Instead workers were encouraged to join works committees and work through government appointed structures to resolve disputes.

  Black workers rejected this system of control. By 1960 only ten works committees had been formed in the whole of South Africa!

- **no Wage Board hearings for African trade unions**

  In 1955, African trade unions were no longer allowed to sit at Wage Board hearings and lost the important right to call for and influence wage determinations.

- **no stop orders for African trade unions**

  In 1959, the Bantu Labour Act was amended and it became illegal for African trade unions to receive stop orders.

- **no racially mixed trade unions**

  The Industrial Conciliation Amendment Act of 1956 provided the major obstacle to the development of a united non-racial trade union movement in the 1950s.

  This Act amended the 1924 Industrial Conciliation Act and forced the registered trade unions to divide along racial lines.

Main Points of the Industrial Conciliation Amendment Act of 1956

1. No racially 'mixed' (White, Indian and Coloured) trade unions could be registered under the Act.

2. Any existing mixed union was forced to separate into separate unions for each race if more than half of either White, Coloured or Indian membership felt that this was necessary.

3. If these unions did not do this, they had to split into separate racial branches, with separate meetings and only Whites could serve on the executives of the different branches.

4. The Minister had the right to delcare any industry an essential service and prohibit workers from striking in that industry.

5. No trade union would be allowed to affiliate to any political party or take part in elections.

6. The Minister of Labour had the power to reserve any job for a particular race.

This cartoon shows how the Industrial Conciliation Amendment Act protected the rights of White workers and White trade unions.

By the end of the 1940s, the trade union movement was divided. The largest federation, the SATLC, also split into different groups.

In the 1950s, the trade union movement failed to build a united and organised response to these attacks by the government and bosses. As a result, the trade union movement had been severely weakened by the mid-1960s.

3. Trade Union Politics in the 1950s

As a result of the divisions and splits in the 1940s, three clear groupings developed in the trade union movement during the 1950s.

1. White industrial trade unions supported government policy and did everything in their power to safeguard the privileges of their White membership. These racist trade unions united under the South African Confederation of Labour (SACL).

Break up of the SATLC:

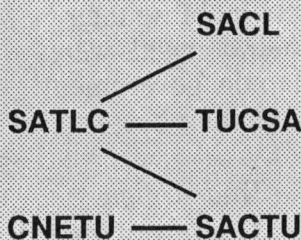

SACL

SATLC —— TUCSA

CNETU —— SACTU

2. The trade unions which came together and formed the Trade Union Council of South Africa (TUCSA), and the Federation of Free African Trade Unions (FOFATUSA). These trade union groupings observed government legislation when it served their interests, and were critical of the government when they needed the support of African workers. Both TUCSA and FOFATUSA argued that trade unions should concern themselves only with issues around wage bargaining and working conditions.

3. The smallest trade union co-ordinating body in this time was the South African Congress of Trade Unions (SACTU). Despite its size, SACTU organised workers non-racially and had the biggest impact on the organisation of African workers. SACTU was a major advance for trade union struggle in South Africa. It argued that politics and economics could not be separated in the working class struggle against exploitation and oppression. It worked in alliance with other political organisations in attempting to do this.

The South African Confederation of Labour

In 1957, the South African Confederation of Labour (SACL) united White racist unions representing over 145 000 members in a single co-ordinating body. The SACL was made up of unions who were members from the Co-ordinating Council of South African Trade Unions (CCSATU), the South African Federation of Trade Unions (SAFTU), and the Federal Consultative Council of SAR&H Staff Associations.

For the first time in the history of the South African working class, racist industrial unions in the railways, mining and steel industries combined to protect the interests of their White members.

SA TRADE UNION CO-ORDINATING BODIES IN 1958

	Membership
SACL	145 000
TUCSA	183 400
SACTU	20 000
Unaffiliated	75 907

The SACL said that the living standards of White workers could only be maintained through racial segregation in the factory and throughout the whole of society. They argued that White workers could keep their jobs only if their jobs were not threatened by African workers.

At times these unions were willing to mobilise their members to strike to ensure that their demands were met. At the same time they turned to the government to help them win racist demands from their bosses.

Throughout the 1950s and 1960s, the Trade Union Council of South Africa (TUCSA) was the largest trade union co-ordinating body. It was made up of conservative unions which had been affiliated to the SATLC. These unions continued to give Black workers second class status in their structures.

The Trade Union Council of South Africa

From the start, trade unions in TUCSA made it clear that they wanted to control African trade unions to protect their own Coloured, Indian and White membership. For this reason, TUCSA tried to control the wage rate through the 'rate for the job' strategy.

TUCSA argued that trade unions should make sure that a wage rate for each job category was set and that no one could be employed below these rates. This demand ensured that the bosses would not be able to employ African workers at lower wages than organised Coloured, Indian and White workers.

At times, TUCSA supported increases in African wages. They usually did this for one of the following reasons:

- The wages of skilled and semi-skilled workers were worked out in relation to the wages of unskilled workers. So, a rise in African wages would lead to a rise in the wages of skilled and semi-skilled workers.

- TUCSA had reformist ideas on how to improve conditions in South Africa. They thought that a rise in African wages would increase the internal market and generate economic growth. This would mean an improvement for all workers.

TUCSA never took a principled stand on the position of African trade unions. They had a shifting racial policy which allowed them to make decisions which best served their members' interests. This policy was guided by one main principle: the need to control African workers.

Parallelism: TUCSA and African Trade Unions

TUCSA tried to stop the growth of a militant Black trade union movement. They tried to incorporate African trade unions into bureaucratic collective bargaining procedures.

African trade unions were excluded from affiliating to TUCSA but were incorporated through liaison committees. This policy adopted by TUCSA was known as 'parallelism'.

African trade unions had the right to 'consult' with the TUCSA executive on issues affecting African workers only. It was expected that the registered TUCSA unions would negotiate on behalf of African workers after they had been consulted.

Attempts to form parallel unions were made in the clothing, textile, catering, food and canning industries.

Most African trade unions rejected these attempts at control. In 1962, TUCSA allowed African trade unions to affiliate. But by 1966, only seven African unions affiliated. At most, there were only 4 000 African members of TUCSA.

There had always been a lot of debate within TUCSA about allowing African unions to affiliate. In 1968, TUCSA expelled African unions. But after the 1973 strikes and growing militancy of African workers, TUCSA once again allowed African unions to affiliate in 1974.

The Federation of Free African Trade Unions

In 1959, the Federation of Free African Trade Unions of South Africa (FOFATUSA) was formed. This had been largely the work of Lucy Mvubelo, a former SACTU unionist and head of the Garment Workers Union of African Women. This union joined with the South African Clothing Workers Union to form the National Union of Clothing Workers (NUCW). The NUCW was the most powerful body within the FOFATUSA.

Other unions within FOFATUSA included the African Motor Workers Union, the African Tobacco Workers Union. Jacob Nyaose, a member of the Pan-Africanist Congress (PAC)* was the first president.

Pan-Africanist Congress (PAC) – the PAC split from the ANC in 1959. They believed in Africanism and that the ANC was not fulfilling the Programme of Action adopted in 1959.

Although FOFATUSA wanted to separate political and economic struggle, in March 1960 Jacob Nyaose promised that all affiliates would strike in support of the PAC's Positive Action Campaign. (During the campaign, the PAC encouraged Africans to leave their pass books at home and report to the nearest police station.) FOFATUSA was established and supported by TUCSA as it provided the Council with some claim to represent African workers.

The anti-communist International Confederation of Free Trade Unions (ICFTU) also played a large role in establishing FOFATUSA.

FOFATUSA was never a very strong trade union body and had collapsed by 1965.

In the 1950s, African trade unions had one of two options:
— They could join TUCSA and perhaps make small economic gains and avoid police repression.
— They could join the South African Congress of Trade Unions (SACTU) which was political, non-racial and far more militant. But it also had to face the full might of the bosses and the government.
Many workers chose the second path.

The South African Congress of Trade Unions

In opposition to the talks set up to establish TUCSA, the CNETU organised a conference of African trade unions to discuss unity. In May 1954, these unions met to discuss ways of resisting the proposed IC Act.

Eventually fourteen unions broke away from the SATLC. Together with the existing CNETU unions, they formed the South African Congress of Trade Unions (SACTU).

Delegates at the inaugural congress of SACTU – 1955

The inaugural congress of SACTU was held in March 1955. It had nineteen affiliates and claimed to represent 20 000 workers. SACTU's membership rose steadily from this time.

In 1959 it claimed to have a membership of 46 000 with an affiliated membership of 35 unions. In 1961, 51 unions (representing 53 000 workers) were affiliated to SACTU.

At its first conference held in Johannesburg in 1956, SACTU spelt out its position very clearly:

'SACTU is conscious of the fact that the organising of the mass of workers for higher wages, better conditions of life and labour is inextricably bound up with a determined struggle for political rights and liberation from all oppressive laws and practices. It follows that a mere struggle for economic rights of all workers without participation in the general struggle for political emancipation would condemn the trade union movement to uselessness and to a betrayal of the interests of the workers.'

In the next two chapters we will see how SACTU tried to put this position into practice.

Chapter Eight
Organise or Starve:
SACTU in the 1950s

SACTU was first and foremost a co-ordinating body for trade unions. It accepted both registered and unregistered trade unions.

The major industrial strength of SACTU came from three registered trade unions: the Food and Canning Workers Union (FCWU) and the African Food and Canning Workers Union (AFCWU), the Textile Workers Industrial Union (TWIU) and the National Union of Laundry, Cleaning and Dyeing Workers (NULCDW).

To remain registered, these unions had to make some changes to their constitutions. This was seen as a tactical decision, and much effort was put into trying to ensure that the unions operated non-racially despite these changes imposed on them.

But even this was not enough for the bosses and government. In the 1950s, they brutally smashed the gains which these unions had made.

Besides the registered industrial unions SACTU, as a co-ordinating body of trade unions, also tried to build industrial unions. Although this was not successful, SACTU established a number of different committees to help build industry-based unions.

This chapter discusses these worker struggles during the 1950s and early 1960s and is divided into the following two sections:

1. **Smashing the Non-Racial Registered Trade Unions**

2. **The Struggle to Build Industrial Unions**

1. Smashing the Non-Racial Registered Trade Unions

The Food and Canning Workers Union and the African Food and Canning Workers Union

The FCWU and the AFCWU were the largest trade unions in SACTU. In 1962 the FCWU/AFCWU had a total membership of over 17 500 workers. At this time there were 23 unions affiliated to SACTU with a total membership of 43 302.

FCWU – Union document from the 1950s:

'Let us not forget that our union branches have a great deal of work to carry out, not only in their **main** task of protecting the interests of the workers in the factories, but also in improving the general standard of life and culture. Our aim must be to make every branch a leader of the community and a centre of social activities....'

'Our union must become a means to a new outlook; a way of fighting poverty, disease and drunkeness, of spreading knowledge and enlightenment and so strengthening the class in its struggle for justice and decency.'

Officials of the FCWU/AFCWU

Non-Racialism and the FCWU/AFCWU

The Food and Canning Workers Union (FCWU) was formed as a non-racial industrial trade union in Cape Town in January 1941. The membership consisted mostly of Coloureds, with a smaller number of Africans and a few Whites.

The African Food and Canning Union (AFCWU) was formed after the government threatened to withdraw the FCWU registration in the 1940s.

Although the unions were separated by law, they worked very closely. Joint committee meetings and annual conferences were held, even after they were prohibited by the 1956 Industrial Conciliation Act.

Conciliation Board – a government-created body which is meant to settle disputes in an industry.

The FCWU sat on Conciliation Boards*, but it also negotiated for the AFCWU. Demands to be taken to the Conciliation Board were decided at general meetings attended by members from both unions.

The FCWU Central Executive Committee, did not discuss the organisational matters of the AFCWU branches. This was done at special meetings of the AFCWU. The National Executive Committee meetings of the FCWU dealt with overlapping matters of the two unions, but not the specific affairs of the AFCWU

The Bosses and the Government Move Against the Union

In the early 1950s, the food and canning industry grew very quickly. The FCWU/AFCWU were able to secure a number of gains for their members during this time.

But in the second half of the 1950s profits in the food industry fell because of increasing competition in overseas markets.

The bosses now changed their attitude. Together with the government they smashed the union!

With profits falling in the food and canning industry,

the larger companies began to take control of more and more of the industry.

In 1955, the LKB (Langeberg Ko-operatiewe Beperking) took over four large canning companies and now had ten factories under its control. In 1956, SA Dried Fruit also took control of a number of companies.

Management tried as hard as possible to smash the union. Worker leaders were victimised and fired for being 'inefficient'. Stop-orders were withdrawn and only provided to the FCWU after much protest.

In 1958 the Wage Board recommended a cut in wages in the food industry. The next year, the government declared the canning industry an essential service*, and took away the right to strike.

essential service – in South Africa the government has the right to declare a sector of industry an 'essential service'. The government sees this sector as essential to the maintenance of the economy and limits are placed on industrial action.

In 1959, LKB implemented a cut in wages. Workers went on strike in the Port Elizabeth factory and a national boycott of LKB products was called. The company was forced to pay the old wage rate.

In the 1960s, the union was severely weakened. Union leaders were arrested and banned. Workers were retrenched as new machinery was brought into the factory. A number of factories were also closed down.

So while production was speeded up, and profits re-established, many workers lost their jobs in the food and canning industry. In these years, the early militancy of the FCWU and the AFCWU was lost. It only to re-emerged in the 1970s.

The Textile Workers Indutrial Union and the Amato Textile Mills Strike

Amato textile workers of the TWIU being baton charged by the police while on strike in 1958

One of the most important strikes in the 1950s was at the Amato Textile Mills in Benoni in February 1958. This strike over higher wages lasted for three days. On the third day it was broken up by about 100 policemen who attacked the striking workers after they had marched 17 km from Daveyton to gather outside the factory.

The TWIU was a very powerful union within the Transvaal region of SACTU. Over 4 000 workers were employed at the Amato textile factory. In Benoni there were no other factories which employed more than 1 000 workers.

In the whole of the Transvaal, SACTU had only 15 000 organised members by 1958. So the workers organised at Amato accounted for over 25% of SACTU's membership in the region.

Compared to other factories in the 1950s, Amato was well organised. There were over 50 shop stewards who met once a week.

After the workers began pressurising management for higher pay, the company offered increases only to some departments. The workers held a general meeting and decided they should strike.

The government responded by attacking the union in the factory. On the third day of the strike the police dispersed the workers. 340 workers were blacklisted and were unable to get jobs. Many were forced to return to the bantustans* because of influx control legislation.

bantustans – homelands – a dumping ground for workers and their families when industry does not need them.

The union in the factory was smashed.

The FCWU and the TWIU were two registered trade union affiliates of SACTU. They had existed before SACTU and were well-established trade unions.

SACTU however, wanted to organise as many workers into industrial trade unions as possible.

To try and organise workers in these industries, SACTU developed a number of organisational structures. These included:

- *Local Committees (LC)*
- *National Organising Committees (NOC), and a*
- *General Workers Union (GWU)*

2. The Struggle to Build Industrial Unions

Local Committees

Local Committees were established in the major industrial centres to help organise workers into industrial unions. Workers would first be organised into Local Committees.

The National Executive Committee of SACTU had the power to establish or disband these committees.

The stronger committees were usually in those cities

where the registered SACTU unions provided financial support.

The first local committee was set up in **Johannesburg**. But membership on the Witwatersrand remained at 15 000 and few stable unions were established between 1956 and 1961.

Witwatersrand Workers' Council of Action Conference – 1954

The Witwatersrand LC was badly hit by police arrests. The brutal crushing of the strike at the Amato Textile Mills was a major blow to SACTU organisation in this area.

In **Cape Town**, the LC drew heavily on the resources of the Food and Canning Workers Union (FCWU). In this area members of the ANC worked for SACTU and played a large role in organising workers.

During the 1940s, in **Port Elizabeth**, seven trade unions were formed in the cement, soft drinks, food and canning, engineering, leather and distributive industries. Worker committees and a central trade union office were established for the unions.

This organisation helped strengthen the unions during the 1950s.

As in Cape Town, the leadership of the trade unions in the Eastern Cape was closely linked to the leadership of other political organisations.

In 1956, six new unions were formed in the Eastern Cape.

In **Durban** and **Natal,** SACTU had major organisational successes. In addition to the Durban Local Committee, new Local Committees were formed in Pinetown, Ladysmith and Pietermaritzburg during 1959.

The Durban Local Committee was formed with nine unions in 1955. Between 1959 and 1960 SACTU's membership in Durban increased by over 5 000 members.

The South African Railway and Harbour Workers Union organised by the Durban LC claimed a membership of around 3 500, making it the largest transport workers' union in South Africa.

SARH Workers Union, Transvaal

Before 1958, efforts to organise metal, transport and dock workers were in the hands of the Local Committees. After 1958, special National Organising Committees (NOCs) were created for workers in agriculture, transport, metal and mining industries.

National Organising Committees

The main aim of the National Organising Committees (NOCs) was to co-ordinate activities and establish a national union for transport, metal, mining and farm workers.

Conditions in the 1950s made this very difficult, but real attempts were made to form national unions in these industries.

1. Transport Industry

The Transport National Organising Committee (NOC) worked amongst railway, dock and bus workers. At the time, different trade unions organised workers on the docks, railways and the buses. Even these trade unions were usually only in one area and did not unite nationally.

As a result, the NOC concerned itself with general demands and acted as a pressure group by preparing memorandums on wage rates and working committees. They submitted these to the Minister of Transport and other Members of Parliament.

2. Metal Industry

The metal NOC included metal unions from Port Elizabeth, the Transvaal and Cape Town.

In 1962, the NOC for the metal industry prepared a memorandum on conditions in the industry. The report was eventually submitted to the industrial council for the metal industry.

The attempt to form a National Union of Metal Workers was proposed and endorsed at a number of conferences, but never achieved.

By 1963, all SACTU organisers in the metal industry had been either banned or detained and this made organising very difficult.

3. Mining Industry

Since the crushing of the 1946 mineworkers' strike, mine bosses made it very difficult for workers to organise trade unions.

The mining NOC tried to recruit volunteers and co-opt leaders of other SACTU unions to distribute pamphlets on the weekends near mining compounds. These activists were often intimidated by the police.

By November 1961, SACTU had only managed to attract a total paid up membership of 100 mineworkers.

Faced with these difficulties, the SACTU NOC for mining produced propaganda and prepared memorandums about the harsh conditions facing workers on the mines.

4. Agriculture

In the 1950s, farmworkers made up about one third of South Africa's working class, but had fewer legal rights than workers in the cities.

Conditions for farm workers on the capitalist farms were very bad at this time. Workers were paid very low wages and were often assaulted by their bosses.

In 1959 SACTU resolved to build a NOC for agriculture. In the same year SACTU took a leading role in organising the 'Potato Boycott' called by the ANC.

The boycott was called to highlight the conditions of workers on potato farms. Hundreds of thousands of people refused to buy potatoes, and the boycott was only called off at the end of the potato season.

By 1961, SACTU formed the Farm, Plantation and Allied Workers Union (FPAWU). This union was only organised in the Transvaal, although there were attempts to organise workers in the Cape and in Natal. By early 1962, the union had grown to over 1 000 members.

The union took up a number of legal cases on behalf of individual workers over assault and eviction issues.

Both the Local Committees and the National Organising Committees strengthened workers industrially in their struggle against the bosses and the government. In 1961, SACTU formed General Workers Unions to help build industrial unions.

General Workers Unions

The General Workers Unions (GWU) were to 'temporarily accommodate' unorganised workers until they could be placed in industrial unions.

The success of and the way that these GWUs fitted into the structure of SACTU differed from area to area.

In Kimberley a GWU was formed in 1955. It had very close relations with the SACTU head office in the Witwatersrand. In 1960, it had 700 members and was allowed to affiliate directly to SACTU.

Other GWUs were formed under the supervision of the Local Committees. They could not form executive committees.

In 1955 a GWU was established under the Durban Local Committee. Most of the workers who joined SACTU between 1959 and 1960 in Durban were included in the GWU and went on to form the South African Railways and Harbour Workers Union. In 1962, there were 2 000 workers in the Durban GWU.

The Cape Town and Witwatersrand local committees were not very happy about forming these general unions. They were afraid that they would be too loosely organised. Despite this, both centres established GWUs in 1960. By 1962, they had each enrolled about 400 members.

In Port Elizabeth, a GWU was established in 1960 and had 674 members by 1962.

SACTU's attempts to form industrial unions on a national scale were not very successful although some unity had been achieved within each industry. Organisers were working under very difficult conditions. The bosses and the government acted very harshly against worker organisations. The levels of development of capitalism also effected the way that workers could organise. It placed limits on worker organisation. Workers usually worked in small factories in different parts of the country. This made national organisation much more difficult.

It was only in the 1960s and 1970s that this position was to change in any major way.

But SACTU's power and politics did not end on the factory floor. With little support coming from the registered trade unions, workers in SACTU tried to increase their power by taking up joint campaigns with other organisations in the Congress Alliance.

S.A. CONGRESS OF TRADE UNIONS

AN INJURY TO ONE IS AN INJURY TO ALL

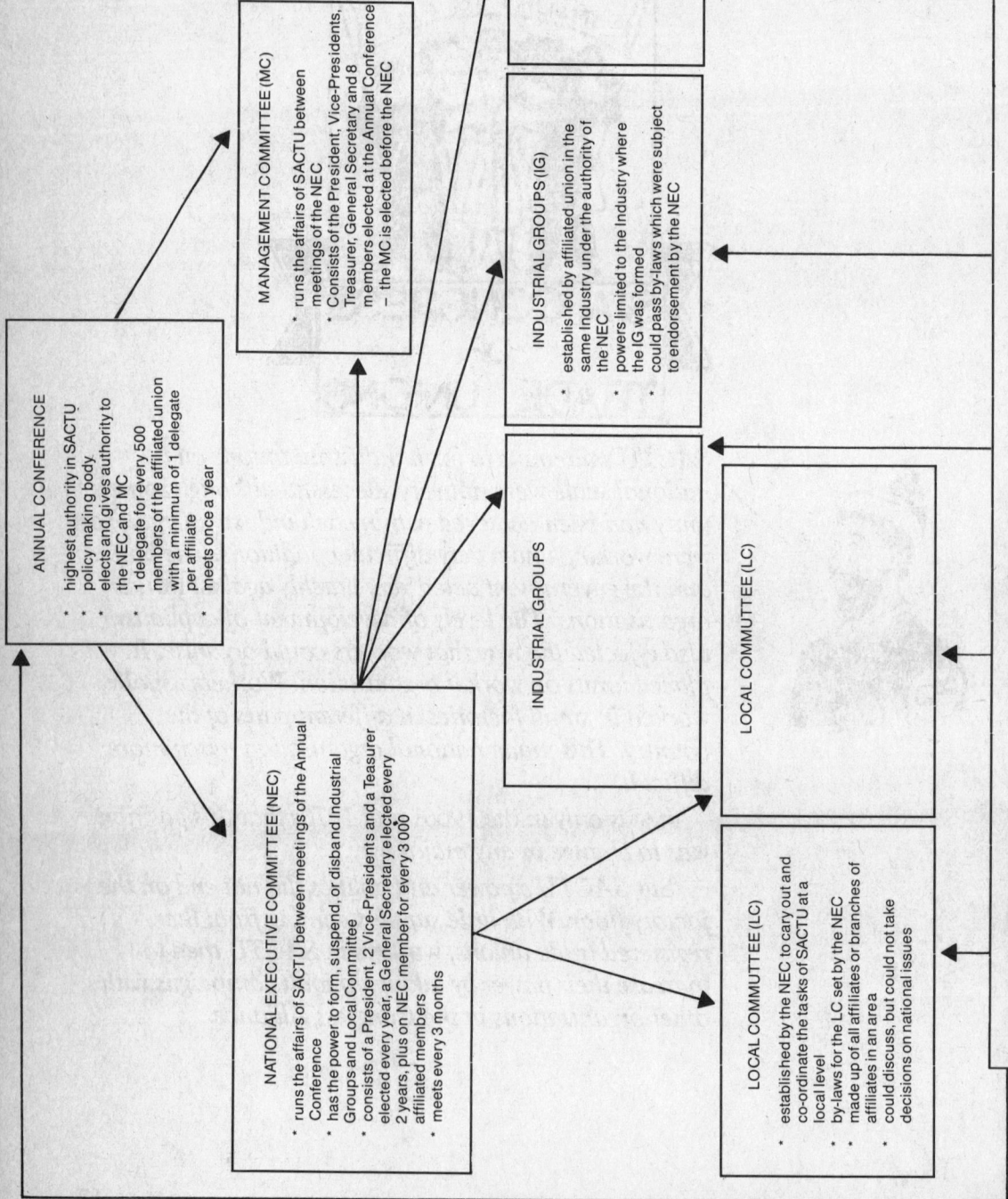

ANNUAL CONFERENCE
* highest authority in SACTU
* policy making body
* elects and gives authority to the NEC and MC
* 1 delegate for every 500 members of the affiliated union with a minimum of 1 delegate per affiliate
* meets once a year

MANAGEMENT COMMITTEE (MC)
* runs the affairs of SACTU between meetings of the NEC
* Consists of the President, Vice-Presidents, Treasurer, General Secretary and 8 members elected at the Annual Conference – the MC is elected before the NEC

NATIONAL EXECUTIVE COMMITTEE (NEC)
* runs the affairs of SACTU between meetings of the Annual Conference
* has the power to form, suspend, or disband Industrial Groups and Local Committee
* consists of a President, 2 Vice-Presidents and a Treasurer elected every year, a General Secretary elected every 2 years, plus on NEC member for every 3 000 affiliated members
* meets every 3 months

INDUSTRIAL GROUPS (IG)

INDUSTRIAL GROUPS (IG)
* established by affiliated union in the same Industry under the authority of the NEC
* powers limited to the Industry where the IG was formed
* could pass by-laws which were subject to endorsement by the NEC

INDUSTRIAL GROUPS

LOCAL COMMITTEE (LC)

LOCAL COMMITTEE (LC)
* established by the NEC to carry out and co-ordinate the tasks of SACTU at a local level
* by-laws for the LC set by the NEC
* made up of all affiliates or branches of affiliates in an area
* could discuss, but could not take decisions on national issues

AFFILIATES OF SACTU

Chapter Nine
SACTU and the Congress Alliance

SACTU did not hide its political position.

Three months after it was formed, SACTU sent delegates to the Congress of the People organised by the Congress Alliance. Later that year, it became a formal member of the Congress Alliance with representation on the National Co-ordinating Committee.

The Congress Alliance was not the first attempt to build unity in the struggle against oppression in South Africa and was born out of many years of protest and challenge.

As an affiliate, SACTU was actively involved in a number of the Congress Alliance's political campaigns. At times, it was SACTU which initiated and took on the main organising role for these campaigns.

Despite this, by the mid-1960s SACTU had suffered a number of severe setbacks. It hardly existed as an organised trade union centre in South Africa, but it had established an external mission.

SACTU did however leave a mark on the South African working class which was never to fade: the struggle to unite the political and economic struggles of the working class.

This chapter looks at these developments in the 1950s and 1960s, and is divided into the following parts:

1. **Early Attempts at Unity**

2. **The Origins of the Congress Alliance – 1920s to the 1950s**

3. **The Congress Alliance: Mass Protest and Police Repression – the 1950s and 1960s**

4. **SACTU and the Stayaway Campaigns**

5. **SACTU and the Campaign of Economic Sabotage**

The Congress Alliance was an alliance of a number of different organisations:

- The African National Congress (ANC)
- The South African Indian Congress (SAIC)
- The South African Congress of Democrats (SACOD)
- The South African Coloured Peoples Organisation (SACPO)

SACTU was the only organisation in the Congress Alliance which had a non-racial constitution. It represented the non-racial trade union movement in the alliance.

But before the 1950s, many attempts had been made to unite the struggle of workers with all the oppressed in South Africa.

During the 1920s, 1930s and 1940s a number of organisations co-operated with each other around particular campaigns.

1. Early Attempts at Unity

Non-European Unity Conferences – 1927 to 1934

Non-European Unity Conferences were held in 1927, 1930, 1931 and 1934. These conferences included delegates from the APO, ANC, ICU as well as Indian representatives. Black grievances were discussed and a number of resolutions were passed recording opposition to government policy.

At the 1930 conference, a resolution was passed to establish a more permanent organisation to co-ordinate Black political activity. This however never came about. This was largely due to the fear of some organisations that they may lose their independence in forming such an organisation.

The next major attempt to forge unity between different organisations was the formation of the All African Convention (AAC) in 1935.

The All African Convention: 1935 to 1942

The All African Convention (AAC) was formed in response to the proposed passing of the Hertzog Bills which were a fresh assault on African rights relating to the land, labour and the vote.

The AAC met in 1935, 1936 and in 1937 it was declared a permanent organisation to meet once every three years. A constitution was adopted. The organisation had a federal structure in which the independence of individual affiliates was safeguarded.

Co-ordinating committees in particular areas were to be established, with two or three representatives from each affiliated organisation. These committees would deal with issues which arose in the district.

The Ten Point Programme – a minimum programme drawn up by the Anti-CAD (Coloured Affairs Department) and delegates from the All Africa Convention who formed the Non-European Unity Movement (NEUM) in 1943. It was to act as a basis for principled unity with any organisation which wished to join the Non-European Unity Movement.

From the start the AAC faced many problems. First, there were tensions between the ANC and the AAC.

By 1935 the ANC was beginning to revive itself, and in December it resolved that the AAC had 'fulfilled its useful purpose' and 'should now cease to function and merge in the ANC'.

In December 1943 a joint committee meeting was held between representatives of the ANC and AAC. Although this meeting decided that the AAC would be 'the official mouthpiece of the Africans', the decision was rejected by a conference of the ANC who refused to affiliate.

Arising from the AAC, the Non-European Unity Movement (NEUM) was formed in 1943 and adopted the Ten Point Programme* as a basis of unity.

In the meantime, the 1940s saw closer co-operation around a number of campaigns between those organisations which were later to form the Congress Alliance.

Delegates at a joint meeting of the ANC and APO in 1931. This meeting helped prepare the way for the All African Convention in 1935.

2. The Origins of the Congress Alliance – 1920s to the 1950s

In the 1920s and 1930s The African National Congress, The South African Indian Congress, the Communist Party of South Africa, African Peoples Organisation and different women's organisations, often jointly resisted government repression and legislation.

In 1947 the 'Doctors' Pact' was signed between Dr Naicker, Dr Dadoo and Dr Xuma. The Pact was a declaration of co-operation between the ANC, the Natal Indian Congress (NIC) and the Transvaal Indian Congress (TIC).

On May Day in 1950, there was a joint call by the ANC and other organisations for workers to stay away from work. The stayaway was to protest against the banning and detention of many leading communists and trade unionists.

With the help of the Council for Non-European Trade Unions (CNETU), the stayaway was effective on the Witwatersrand.

The police however, responded violently. Gatherings were broken up in townships in Benoni, Orlando, Alexandra, Sophiatown and Brakpan. Rioting followed, nineteen people were killed and over 30 left injured.

On 14 May 1950, representatives from the executive committees of the ANC, SAIC, APO, ANC Youth League, Communist Party and the Transvaal Council of Non-European Trade Unions (TCNETU), pledged to take immediate steps to mobilise mass opposition to the passing of the Unlawful Organisations Bill.

On 21 May, the national executive of the ANC called for a 'National Day of Protest and Mourning' to serve 'as a day of mourning for all those Africans who lost their lives in the struggle for liberation' and to oppose new government laws.

A committee which included representatives of the ANC and SAIC was established to co-ordinate the activities. A stayaway was called for 26 June and was most successful among workers in Port Elizabeth and Durban.

These campaigns and stayaways in the early 1950s, laid the foundations for the Defiance Campaign in 1952.

The 1952 Defiance Campaign

The committee which was established to co-ordinate the activities of the stayaway in June, led to the creation of a Joint Planning Council. This was a five-person council made up of executive members of the ANC and the SAIC and was to look into ways of mounting a campaign against recently passed laws.

After failing to have the six unjust laws repealed, the executives of the ANC, SAIC and FRAC (Franchise Action Committee) called for a Defiance Campaign to begin on 26 June 1952. The Defiance Campaign was a campaign of civil disobedience. People were meant to defy government laws in a peaceful way.

The campaign opened in Port Elizabeth and on the Witwatersrand.

The laws broken were minor ones and included Blacks using White facilities, such as railway stations, trains and post offices. Curfew laws and pass regulations were also disobeyed. People also entered African locations without permits.

The campaign spread across a number of cities and reached its peak in September 1952. In that month 2 500 people were arrested in 24 different towns and cities. Throughout the whole campaign over 8 000 people were arrested.

Between October and November however, the campaign came to a standstill. Rioting broke out in East London and Port Elizabeth. The police moved in. Curfews were imposed and a number of people were banned.

Fordsburg 1952 –
The Defiance Campaign
is launched.

143

Despite the initial success of the campaign, the Joint Planning Council argued that there would have to be more organisation in future campaigns and that future campaigns should 'arise from the concrete conditions under which people live.'

These suggestions led up to the formation of the Congress Alliance and the adoption of the Freedom Charter at the Congress of the People in 1955.

3. The Congress Alliance: Mass Protest and Police Repression – the 1950s and 1960s

In 1953, ZK Matthews of the ANC set the ball rolling when he suggested the idea of calling a 'national convention at which all groups might be represented to consider our national problems on an all-inclusive basis' and to 'draw up a Freedom Charter for the democratic South Africa of the future'.

The Congress of the People and the Freedom Charter

In March 1954, the executives of the ANC, SAIC, SACOD, and SACPO met and decided to establish a National Action Council (NAC) for the Congress of the People. This council would consist of eight delegates from each of the organisations involved.

A national organiser was appointed to ensure that the campaign got off the ground. SACTU joined the NAC in 1955.

When the campaign for the drawing up of the Freedom Charter was announced, a call was made for 10 000 volunteers to help collect demands and organise for the Congress of the People.

A common way of collecting demands was for one person to record suggestions at meetings or to collect written suggestions. These were summarised and sent to a regional committee of the National Action Council.

A number of subcommittees broke the demands into different categories, and the Freedom Charter was eventually drafted by a committee of the NAC and reviewed by the National Executive of the ANC on the eve of the Congress.

The Congress of the People held in Kliptown near Johannesburg in 1955, was attended by over 3 000 delegates from all over the country.

Kliptown 1955 – Delegates at the Congress of the People

At the congress, the various clauses of the Freedom Charter were introduced and they were followed by impromptu speeches from the audience. After these speeches, the clauses of the Freedom Charter were read out aloud and passed by a show of hands.

A 'million signature' campaign was launched to popularise the Freedom Charter in South Africa, and about 100 000 signatures were collected under conditions of severe police harassment.

The platform at the Congress of the People

The Congress Alliance however, did not limit itself to the drawing up of the Freedom Charter. The alliance actively campaigned around different sets of demands against the government. SACTU was often at the centre of these campaigns.

4. SACTU and the Stayaway Campaigns

1957 Stayaway: Pound-a-day Campaign

In the first months of 1957 SACTU organised a National Workers' Conference. At this conference over 300 trade union delegates decided to mobilise a national campaign for a minimum wage of a pound-a-day. The campaign set out to achieve three basic aims:

- SACTU wanted to increase the wages of the working class.

- There had been a number of bus boycotts around Johannesburg and Port Elizabeth. SACTU wanted to build on this working class activity.

- The campaign was meant to act as a way of signing up workers into trade unions.

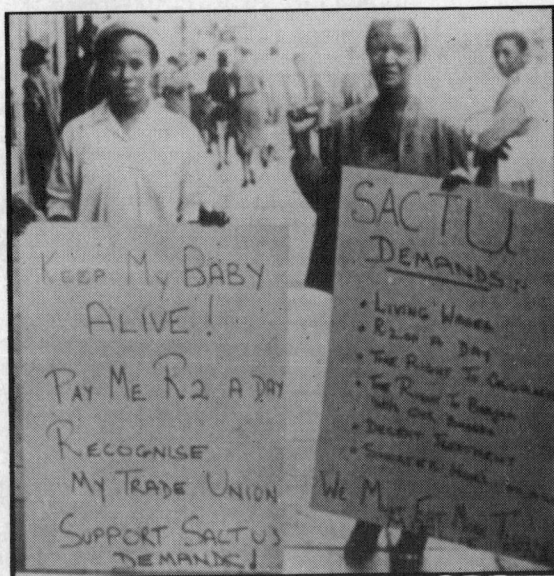

Workers hold a placard demonstration demanding a pound a day.

The campaign had the support of the Congress Alliance and started with a call for workers in Port Elizabeth and Johannesburg to stay away from work on 26 June. Strike committees were established in these areas and pamphlets urged workers to strike for a pound-a-day minimum wage.

In Johannesburg, Vereeniging and Port Elizabeth it was estimated that 70 to 80% of workers stayed away from work.

This demonstration, together with the earlier working class action around industrial and political disputes from 1955 to 1957, had an effect on workers' wages. In 1958 the government recommended a number of wage determinations. Real wages for workers rose in that year.

147

1958 Stayaway: Pound-a-day and General Elections

In February 1958, SACTU organised a number of regional workers' conferences in the Transvaal, Natal, and the Eastern and Western Cape. These conferences led to a second National Workers' Conference in Newclare in Johannesburg.

1 673 delegates and 3 000 observers attended the conference and decided to call a national strike around two main slogans:

FORWARD TO POUND-A-DAY VICTORY!

THE NATIONALISTS MUST GO!

A three-day national strike was called for the same time as the White election.

In the weeks leading up to the strike, the emphasis on the different demands began to change. The slogan calling for the end of the nationalist government received much more attention from the Congress leadership than the call for a pound-a-day minimum wage.

The police prepared themselves and the employers took precautions before the strike. The police conducted pass raids into the townships in the days before the strike. At 2 am, on the morning of the first day of the strike on 14 April 1958, the police entered the townships in large numbers.

The strike itself was not very successful. On the first day of the strike, only about 10% of workers on the Witwatersrand stayed away from work. In Port Elizabeth about 50% of workers did not go to work and in Durban about 30%.

Oliver Tambo, from the Witwatersrand ANC National Working Committee called the strike off after the first day. SACTU was not consulted in this decision.

There were many reasons why the stayaway was not as great a success as some of the leaders had hoped. Many of the reasons related to the levels of organisation and communication between workers. Another factor was noted by Dan Tloome, a veteran trade unionist at the time. He said that the stress on the slogan of 'The Nationalists must go' led to a great deal of confusion. Many people thought that this meant that the ANC was in favour of the United Party coming to power!

The Nationalist Party increased their majority in the White parliament in these elections but resistance continued.

Sharpeville – the streets after the shooting

1960 Stayaway: National Day of Mourning

After the Sharpeville massacre on 21 March 1960, in which 69 people were killed and over 180 wounded, Chief Albert Lutuli called for a National Day of Mourning on 28 March 1960.

This call for a one day stay-at-home, turned into a prolonged strike with mass marches and rioting in many areas. Most of this action was not carefully organised and planned. The government responded with harsh repression. They declared a State of Emergency.

The ANC and PAC were banned and forced to operate underground. There were a number of arrests and the strikes were crushed.

But this was not the end. In August 1960 the State of Emergency was lifted. Organisational work began again. A National Action Council (NAC) was elected at an 'All-in Africa Conference'. A number of different political organisations were represented at this conference, but members of the ANC were the dominant force.

The aim of the NAC was to explain to the entire population of South Africa 'the true meaning and significance of the campaign for a National Convention'*.

At a meeting on 14 April 1961 a decision was made to call for a three day national strike and demonstration. This was to take place from 29 to 31 May 1961. It was planned to take place at the same time as South Africa was being proclaimed a Republic.

1961 Stayaway: Call for a National Convention

SACTU played a major role in organising for this strike. It was the only effective member of the Congress Alliance which had not been banned. Workers had learnt from the stayaways in the 1950s, and the organisation of the political strike was carefully planned.

The country was zoned into a number of regions. Each region had a full-time organiser. Strike committees were formed in Soweto, the East Rand townships, Alexandra and Sharpeville.

The police responded. A new law, which allowed the government to detain anybody for twelve days without bail, was passed. Over 10 000 Blacks were arrested. There were nightly searches in the townships by the police, and there was a massive display of armed might with tanks, helicopters and armoured cars patrolling.

After the first day of the strike, the daily newspapers claimed that the strike was a failure. On the second day of the protest, Nelson Mandela, secretary of the NAC told workers to return to work as the strike was not successful. He said that this 'closes a chapter in our methods of political struggle.'

Research into the strike by the NAC showed that the 1961 political strike had actually been the most successful worker stayaway over a political issue in the history of South Africa. The NAC report concluded that 'wherever workers were organised into trade unions there was a favourable response to the strike call.'

There was to be a second phase to the campaign. This was to be based on non-co-operation and strengthened industrial organisation of workers. This phase was never implemented.

5. SACTU and the Campaign of Economic Sabotage

With police repression escalating, and the banning of organisations and detention of many leaders, the December 1960 annual conference of the Communist Party, decided to embark upon a campaign of economic sabotage* as a first stage to guerilla war.

economic sabotage – destruction and interference in goods and industry to disrupt the economy.

The Congress Alliance did not immediately support this call. But after the 1961 stayaway many leaders and members of the ANC and SACTU chose a similar path.

A 'national high command' was established at Rivonia to co-ordinate the campaign. This high command worked independently of any existing political organisation.

In June 1961, the National Executive Committee of the ANC agreed to join this program of economic sabotage to lead on to guerilla war.

Umkonto we Sizwe (Spear of the Nation) was formed to carry out this task.

The program of sabotage began on 15 and 16 December 1961. In eighteen months over 200 acts of sabotage were carried out. On 11 June 1963, Umkonto headquarters at Rivonia were raided and Nelson Mandela and many leaders were arrested. The Rivonia Trial began in October.

Under these conditions, the political leadership of the ANC were forced to move outside of South Africa.

The government banned the ANC in 1961, but SACTU was never banned in South Africa. With the involvement of SACTU officials and members in the sabotage campaign, the government identified SACTU with the Congress movement. The leadership came under the attack of the state.

In 1962 the Sabotage Act was passed. This was worded in a way that even strikes could be included as acts of sabotage. Between 1960 and 1966, 160 SACTU officials were arrested and a number of these were convicted on sabotage charges.

The detention, bannings and arrests of SACTU leaders hit the non-racial trade union movement hard.

Much of the organising in the late 1950s had not focussed on building strong and permanent organisational structures. With the leadership joining the armed struggle, and no lasting structures controlled by workers, organisationally, SACTU faded away in South Africa.

SACTU however, did continue to exist. During the 1960 State of Emergency, an external commission of SACTU was formed in different centres around the world. Inside South Africa however, the experience of the SACTU unions in the 1950s and early 1960s was to live on into the next round of democratic trade unionism in the 1970s.

Nelson Mandela

152

Chapter Ten
Profits and Repression:
Workers Resist:
1960s to the early 1970s

With opposition inside the country badly weakened during the 1960s, profits came rolling in for the bosses.

The economy also underwent some major changes. Fewer and fewer large companies now dominated the economy.

But these changes could never have been achieved without the strict controls and repression imposed by the apartheid government. These were the high years of apartheid!

But by the 1970s, things began to change. Once again, workers began to mobilise and organise – to fight back!

This chapter discusses these struggles, and the effects they had on trade unions.

The chapter is divided into the following sections:

1. **Pushing Profits – The Changing Economy in the 1960s**

2. **The Government in Control – Apartheid in the 1960s**

3. **Trade Unions and the Working Class in the 1960s**

4. **Workers Strike Back**

1. Pushing Profits – The Changing Economy in the 1960s

The 1960s were very important years for the development of capitalism in South Africa. The problems which the capitalists faced in the 1950s were temporarily ironed out during the 1960s.

The strong racist government, which crushed all opposition and placed strict controls over the movement of workers, secured conditions for the rapid accumulation of profits.

At the same time, there were major changes in the way that the economy was controlled and structured.

Rapid Growth

GNP – Gross National Product – the total value of goods and services produced within a country, together with the goods and services produced overseas by locally based companies.

Between 1960 and 1970 the South African Gross National Product GNP* increased from about R5 200 million to R12 400 million. The average annual growth rate of the economy was 6%. Together with Japan the South African economy had the highest growth rate in the world.

Monopoly Capitalism

There have always been large monopoly companies in South Africa. From very early on in the history of capitalism in South Africa, the gold and diamond mines had been developed by companies which had monopoly control over the mining sector of the economy.

These monopolies did not control all the major branches of capitalist production. There were still a number of smaller capitalists involved in the important manufacturing sector of the economy.

During the 1960s, the South African economy was being controlled by fewer and fewer capitalists.

The 1977 Monopolies Commission reported that:

i)   5% of the total number of firms in manufacturing accounted for 63% of the sector's turnover.

ii) 5% of those in the wholesale and retail trade accounted for almost 70% of turnover.

iii) 5% of firms in construction accounted for 63% of turnover.

iv) 5% in transport accounted for 73% of turnover.

Phew! This means that in each of the most important sectors of the economy, 5% of the companies controlled more than 60% of the market!

SASOL – making oil from coal and profits from workers

Capital Intensive Industrialisation

The growth of the South African economy in the 1960s was capital intensive*. In the 1930s, the capitalists relied on plenty of cheap labour to make their profits and increase productivity. But the capitalists in the 1960s invested large amounts of money in machinery to speed up productivity.

capital intensive industrialisation – this is the development of industry through the investment of large amounts of money in machinery.

Foreign Investment in the 1960s

Most foreign capital was invested in manufacturing. It has been said that in the 1960s as much as 40% of South African industry was controlled by foreign interests. These were in the key sectors such as chemicals, oil, computers and motor production.

The Parastatals

In the 1960s there was further state investment in the economy, especially in the parastatals. Between 1960 and 1970 the public corporations (ISCOR, ESCOM, SASOL, SATS etc.) increased their share of domestic fixed investment* from 6% to 11%.

domestic fixed investment – the amount of money invested in a country in any one year.

In the second half of the 1960s the parastatals grew even faster than private companies.

So, by the end of the 1960s the South African economy was being controlled more and more by a few monopolies, multinational companies*, and the large parastatals.

multinational companies – these are large companies which operate in a number of different parts of the world and not just in one country.

2. The Government in Control – Apartheid in the 1960s

Throughout the 1960s, the government kept very strict controls over Black people.

Repression

There were very heavy penalties for those people the state thought were furthering the aims of a banned organisation. Many laws were passed which gave the police and military greater powers.

In 1967, the Terrorism Act introduced a new range of offences and provided for indefinite detention. In 1969, the Bureau of State Security was established and huge powers were placed in the hands of cabinet ministers.

Bantustans and Townships

In 1959 the government passed the Promotion of Bantu Self-government Act. This law opened the way to imposing the bantustan system onto millions of Africans in the country.

The Act recognised eight African 'national units' and the powers of local territorial, regional and tribal authorities were clearly defined. This was in preparation for the possibility of self-government, and even full 'independence' of the bantustans.

The bantustan system went hand in hand with the growth of townships and the refusal of the government to recognise that Blacks living in South Africa's cities have any rights.

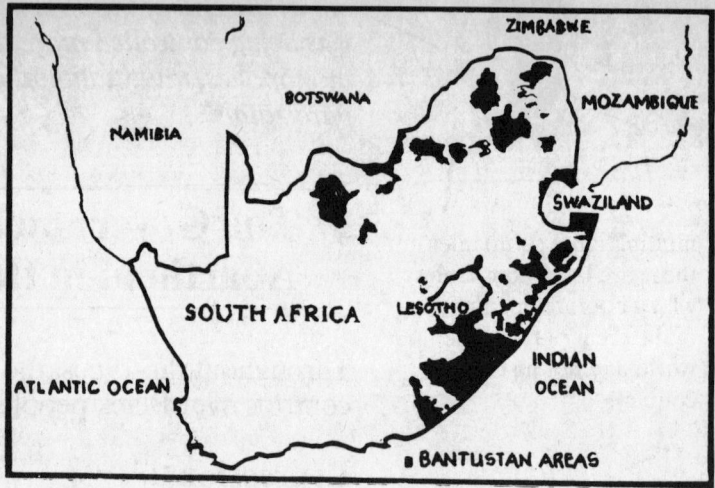

Many townships were built during the 1960s.

During the 1960s massive townships, with very few facilities were built for Africans living in the cities and towns. These townships were built at a very low cost and saved the bosses and the government millions of rands.

The government also tried to reverse the flow of Africans into the cities.

Over one million labour tenants and farm squatters, and 400 000 city dwellers were resettled in the bantustans in the 1960s. The population of the bantustans increased by 70%. A further 327 000 people were brought directly under the control of the bantustan authorities. This happened when townships were incorporated into the neighbouring reserves.

Labour Laws

The Bantu Labour Act of 1964 and the Bantu Labour Regulations of 1965, introduced a whole range of laws which attempted to control workers and send them to places where their labour was most needed.

labour bureaus – offices set up by the government to help control the supply and movement of workers in South Africa.

These regulations and laws established labour bureaus* around the country. In the major urban areas, a system of local labour bureaus under the management of municipal labour officers was established. Where there were no local labour bureaus, a district labour bureau would operate.

In the rural areas, a similar system applied. In 1968 the Bantu Regulations were extended to all bantustan areas. African work seekers and employers had to register with these bureaus.

In addition to these strict controls placed over the movement of workers, African workers were still not recognised as 'employees' in industrial legislation. African workers were still controlled by the harsh collective bargaining procedures which had been set up by the Bantu Labour (Settlement of Disputes) Act in 1953.

liaison committees – factory-based bodies made up of an equal number of management and worker representatives. Worker representatives were nominated, not elected, and the committees had no negotiating power, serving only to 'advise' on worker grievances.

The Bantu Labour Act introduced liaison committees*. These committees were a failure. Only seven of these committees had been formed by the beginning of 1957. In 1973, there were only 24 liaison committees in the whole country.

3. Trade Unions and the Working Class in the 1960s

The 1960s has been seen as a period of quiet for Black working class activity. Between 1955 and 1960, there had been an average of 76 strikes every year. In 1962, there were only 16 strikes, and 17 in 1963. Why did this happen?

The smashing of the non-racial trade union movement had severely weakened working class resistance. During the 1960s the South African working class was still heavily divided. The major trade union co-ordinating bodies included White racist unions, and TUCSA, where African workers had an inferior position.

These conditions, combined with trade union legislation and other repressive legislation, made it extremely difficult for Black workers to resist the power of the bosses and the government.

Breakdown of Trade Union Membership in 1969 According to Race

BREAKDOWN OF TRADE UNION MEMBERSHIP IN 1969 ACCORDING TO RACE

	Whites	Coloureds	Indians	Africans	Total Membership
SACL	183 781	–	–	–	183 781
TUCSA	79 385	77 272	29 820	–	186 478
Unaffiliated	162 854	30 939	2 835	16 040	212 668
Total	426 020	108 212	32 655	16 040	582 927

But the growth of the economy, capital intensive industrialisation and the shift to monopoly capitalism, had very important results for the working class.

- The growth of the economy increased the size and power of the working class. The number of women as a proportion of the industrial labour force also increased from 2% in 1960 to 7% in 1970.

- Capital intensive industry meant far larger factories with greater numbers of workers. It also meant that demands for semi-skilled and supervisory labour increased. The bargaining power of African workers was also strengthened.

- Monopoly capitalism meant that many workers in different factories and different parts of the country could unite and challenge the same boss.

These conditions made the organisation of workers on the factory floor easier. And so workers saw that unions with strong shop floor structures, organised democratically in the large factories, could demand a far bigger share of the profits of the monopoly capitalists and of the wealth of the country as a whole.

When mass strikes broke out in Durban in 1973, the seeds were sown for the development of a new unionism in South Africa. Workers could now organise to control their own lives.

4. Workers Strike Back

Although profits came rolling in for the bosses in the 1960s, workers received a very small share. By the early 1970s, they were no longer willing to accept this.

In December 1971 and January 1972, 20 000 migrant workers went on strike in Namibia. In late 1972, PUTCO drivers in the Transvaal went on strike and received increases of over 30% in wages. They also formed the Transport and Allied Workers Union (TAWU).

In the same year, stevedores at Cape Town docks staged a work to rule campaign. But the most dramatic events in the early 1970s were the mass strikes which shook Durban, and spread to other areas in 1973.

Strikers locked out at Consolidated Textiles in Jacobs, Durban

The 1973 Durban Strikes

The first wave of strikes which hit Natal in 1973 involved over 60 000 workers. During this strike, workers brought Durban to a standstill.

Durban Coronation Brick and Tile

On 9 January, one of the first factories to come out on strike was Coronation Brick and Tile Company, to the north of Durban city.

The original demand of the 2 000 strong Coronation strikers, was for an increase from R8,79 to R20,00 per week in their minimum cash wage. There had not been a rise in the minimum wage in the factory for over five years.

Workers from the Avoca plant of Coronation joined the strikers from the Number 1 plant. Together they held a mass meeting at the factory stadium.

Workers from the Avoca plant marched to the stadium in two long battle columns and when they flocked through the gates they chanted:

'Ufil'umuntu, ufe usadikiza!' (The person is dead, but his spirit lives on!)

So the bosses at Coronation did not know what had happened to them. The bosses and the government blamed workers' legitimate demands on 'communist agitators' and 'intimidation'! But the workers were strong and they increased their demand to a R30,00 increase per week.

The workers rejected representation on the works committee. King Goodwill Zwelethini offered to negotiate on their behalf if the workers returned to work. This did not happen. By 14 January, workers had elected their own wage delegation of eleven workers.

This collective action won workers at Coronation a R2,07 per week rise. Publicity, and their solidarity, set an example to thousands of other workers. As a result many factories came out on strike even before the Coronation strike was settled. Workers were ready to fight for their rights.

Strikes broke out in a number of factories during January. Sometimes workers received small increases. At other times they met with the full force of the police, and received nothing.

Management's stubborn attitude, the government's threats and the harassment and dismissal of their fellow workers, could not stop the workers.

This was near the end of January when the strikes had moved to the Pinetown-New Germany industrial complex.

King Goodwill appeals to Coronation strikers to go back to to work.

The Frame Group

On 25 January, a massive wave of strikes shook the Phillip Frame Textile empire in Pinetown.

There had long been dissatisfaction over wages and working conditions there. At 8 am on 25 January, workers abandoned their machines and massed in an open yard.

Management invited workers by loudhailer to elect a negotiating committee, and to return to work pending the outcome of the talks. The workers refused and restated their demand for a R20,00 per week wage. At the time they were earning a starvation wage of R5,00 to R9,00 per week.

By the following day, Friday, the mass strike had spread to all other Frame Group factories in the area. This affected about 6 000 African workers and hundreds of Indian workers. The strike spread to other large Frame factories, in Durban, Jacobs and Mobeni.

By Monday, management had made an offer of increases ranging from R1,75 to R3,00 per week. This was a resounding victory for workers, and the workers accepted.

In the first week of February, 16 000 African and Indian municipal workers employed by the Durban Corporation went on strike.

Workers in Durban were seeing the power of collective action and mass participation. By the end of January more than 30 firms in Durban had felt this power of the workers.

Workers were no longer accepting starvation wages. They were organising united action. They were getting tough!

Durban Corporation

Many essential services for the city came to a standstill during the strike. Rubbish piled up, gravediggers were

Year	Strikers
1970	3 303
1971	4 196
1972	8 814
1973	98 029
1974	58 975
1975	23 295
1976	26 931
1977	15 091
1978	14 088
1979	17 323
1980	56 286
1981	84 705

on strike, and the marketplace porters refused to handle goods.

The main abattoir also ceased to function and it was now clear that the supply of perishable goods was severely at risk. White scabs were brought in at the market and to clear the streets.

Thousands of workers marched through the city and industrial areas. Riot Squad police were flown in from Pretoria. They patrolled the industrial areas.

According to press reports, about 1 000 workers, many armed with sticks, marched from the City Electricity Department situated in the heart of Durban. The marchers were confronted by a large number of riot police, armed with Sten guns, FN rifles and batons.

The crowd refused to disperse and they were baton charged. 106 workers were arrested and quickly hustled to court on the following day. They were convicted of 'causing a public disturbance'.

Durban 1973 – workers strike back.

The Strikes Spread

In Natal, strikes spread as far as Pietermaritzburg and Port Shepstone. In Hammarsdale, between Durban and Pietermaritzburg, 7 000 workers employed in twelve industries came out on strike in a demand for higher wages.

The battle of the workers in Natal soon spread to the Rand where the miners were in the frontline of the struggles.

The most publicised miners' action occurred in September 1973 at the Western Deep Levels mine at Carltonville near Johannesburg.

Police opened fire on angry Black miners protesting against the rejection of their wage demand. Twelve miners were shot during the strike. In support of the workers' demands, the Lesotho government announced a temporary suspension of all recruiting for the mines.

Between 1972 and 1973, the Anglo American mining giant increased basic monthly wages for Black miners by 70%. The strikes that erupted in 1973 generally ended up with increases of 15 to 18%.

The wave of strikes which began in 1973 continued right through the 1970s, although not on such a large scale. However, a second wave of mass strikes hit the Transvaal in the early 1980s.

Hayibo! These strikes showed that workers were on the move again. But more important than the strikes was that workers were beginning to organise themselves.

Out of the mass action of the early 1970s, emerged a number of new trade unions. These unions grew to become a very powerful force today.

As was the case during the 1973 strikes, these unions were built from below – by the workers themselves.

Chapter Eleven
Ufil' umuntu, Ufe Usadikiza!
Workers in the 1970s

Militancy and strikes were one thing, but workers realised that to increase their power they had to form trade unions.

In the early 1970s, workers organised new unions in different cities and towns around the country, but TUCSA was still the only trade union federation which organised African unions.

The industrial unions built in the 1970s, were built from almost nothing. To control their trade unions, workers began organising all over again. Often they were assisted by service organisations or advice bureaus.

Workers flocked to join the new unregistered trade unions, despite the fact that they were facing government and employer attacks in the factories and the townships by the late 1970s.

This chapter discusses these struggles and is divided into the following sections:

1. **There's No Magic in the Office – TUACC in the 1970s**

2. **The Urban Training Project and the Consultative Committee of Black Trade Unions**

3. **Formation of the General Workers Union**

4. **Rumblings in TUCSA**

5. **Union Battles in the 1970s – The Struggle for Recognition**

6. **Clamping Down – The Government and the Unions**

After 1973, worker action did not just grind to a halt. New trade unions which gave an organisational form to the worker militancy of the early 1970s, emerged.

By 1974 the first industrial unions which grew from the strikes were launched.

1. There's No Magic in the Office – TUACC in the 1970s

In 1972 the General Factory Workers Benefit Fund (GFWBF) was formed with the assistance of various registered unions in TUCSA in Durban.

The GFWBF tried to provide a basis for worker organisation in Natal. They campaigned for worker rights. The GFWBF also made representations to the Wage Board for the wage determinations of new unskilled workers.

But the Benefit Fund had a longer term aim. This was to act as a stepping-stone to the formation of industrial unions.

In 1973 the Metal and Allied Workers Union (MAWU) and the National Union of Textile Workers (NUTW) emerged from the GFWBF. By 1974 these unions had been joined by the Chemical Workers Industrial Union (CWIU) and the Transport and General Workers Union (TGWU).

Together these unions formed the Trade Union Advisory Co-ordinating Committee (TUACC) in October 1973.

By the next year these four unions alone had signed up over 10 000 members. The total signed up membership of the GFWBF stood at 22 000.

In Natal the TUACC Workers' Project grew from the GFWBF. Workers paid a small subscription fee and received individual legal assistance from TUACC.

By keeping contact with the Workers' Project the unions could draw new factories into industrial unions.

In 1978, TUACC had extended into the Transvaal when the Council of Industrial Workers of the Witwatersrand (CIWW) joined the TUACC unions. The CIWW was formed in 1976 out of the Industrial Aid Society (IAS) and the Transvaal branch of MAWU.

The TUACC unions organised themselves through a strong co-ordinating body which:

- was comprised of a majority of worker delegates at every level of decision-making
- controlled resources from all its affiliates
- decided policy for the affiliates.

From the start, TUACC was committed to building non-racial industrial trade unions based on strong factory floor organisation.

TUACC unions sometimes used liaison or works committees as a tactic for organising. After the militancy of early 1970s, these unions began to build strong organisation at the workplace. Shop stewards played key roles in running a number of the day to day affairs of the union.

Liaison committee at a Transvaal metal company

But TUACC was not the only grouping of trade unions to grow in the early 1970s.

2. The Urban Training Project and the Consultative Committee of Black Trade Unions

In the Transvaal the Urban Training Project (UTP), a service organisation, was formed in 1970. Officials who had been organising African workers in TUCSA came together to:

- establish an educational body to publicise the rights of African workers
- assist Africans who wanted to form trade unions.

The UTP stressed that it was not a worker controlled or worker organisation. By the end of 1975, it was servicing ten different African unions. These trade unions grouped themselves into the Consultative Committee of Black Trade Unions (CCOBTU).

The CCOBTU Unions in 1975

- National Union of Clothing Workers (NUCW)
- Sweet, Food and Allied Workers Union (SFAWU)
- Building Construction and Allied Workers Union (BCAWU)
- Commercial, Catering and Allied Workers Union (CCAWUSA)
- Paper, Wood and Allied Workers Union (PWAWU)
- Glass and Allied Workers Union (GAWU)
- Engineering and Allied Workers Union (EAWU)
- South African Chemical Workers Union (SACWU)
- Laundry, Dry Cleaning and Dye Workers Association (LDCDWA)
- Textile Workers Industrial Union (TWIU)

The CCOBTU included parallel unions organised by TUCSA. Within all these unions the principle of Black leadership was stressed.

This co-ordinating body tried to use works and liaison committees and to get their members to turn them into 'union committees'.

Some of the CCOBTU unions established branches outside the Transvaal in Port Elizabeth and Durban. By 1976, the seven UTP serviced unions claimed a signed up membership of over 19 000.

In the Western Cape, workers followed a different strategy. They did not try and form industrial unions, but rather concentrated on building workers' committees in all industries which came together in a General Workers Union.

3. Formation of the General Workers Union

In Cape Town, the Western Province Workers Advice Bureau (WPWAB) was formed in 1972. By 1976 it claimed a 5 000 strong membership.

At first the WPWAB did not try to organise to establish a trade union or trade union co-ordinating body. Instead, the WPWAB encouraged workers to form works committees. These were democratically elected by workers. These works committees had some legal status.

The works committees helped to build a democratic general union. In 1977, the WPWAB handed over control to a controlling committee formed from the committees in the factories.

It changed its name to the Western Province General Workers Union (WPGWU), and then to the General Workers Union (GWU) after it established branches in Port Elizabeth and Durban.

African workers all over South Africa were beginning to build new and democratic trade unions.

But, during the 1970s, TUCSA was still the largest trade union federation. In fact, TUCSA was the largest trade union federation right up until 1985.

But not all workers were happy with TUCSA. By the 1970s, there were rumblings of discontent within TUCSA, especially from the more militant motor unions in the Eastern Cape. Although the membership continued to grow right up until 1983, so did the discontent.

4. Rumblings in TUCSA

TUCSA MEMBERSHIP IN THE 1970s

Year	Membership
1970	184 242
1971	191 972
1972	194 288
1973	197 861
1974	204 003
1975	210 794
1976	236 905
1977	214 470
1978	221 013
1979	258 655
1980	286 555

In 1968, TUCSA expelled African unions after some of its craft unions had disaffiliated in protest against the presence of African unions in the organisation. In 1969, the General Secretary announced that disaffiliations had cost TUCSA 68 000 members and R16 000 a year.

After the upsurge in militancy among African unions in 1973, TUCSA once again admitted African unions who were organised parallel to registered unions. Once again it tried to control African workers.

TUCSA launched five new parallel unions. By 1976 there were eleven parallel African unions. Only the African Food and Canning Workers Union (AFCWU) was not set up by TUCSA.

TUCSA's attitude angered a number of the affiliates. At the 1976 annual conference the National Union of Motor and Rubber Workers of South Africa (NUMARWOSA) put forward a motion that affiliates should deregister and admit African workers.

Of course the motion was not passed, and three months later NUMARWOSA disaffiliated and began to look for ways of building links with the other unions which had grown in the early 1970s.

175

Rely workers confront management.

Workers all over the country were beginning to find a new source of power through unity and action.

The Food and Canning Workers Union and the African Food and Canning Workers Union were revived, and by 1978 it had established branches in Cape Town, East London, Johannesburg, Ashton, Ceres, Paarl, Worcester, Hout Bay and Saldanha Bay.

The struggle to build democratic and worker controlled trade unions was resurfacing. But workers soon found out that there is no easy road to freedom. The government and the bosses did not welcome the unions with open arms. Many hard battles were fought in the 1970s. The gains made for workers were few and far between. The new trade unions had to develop strategies to fight for their right to exist and be recognised – it was a struggle for survival!

5. Union Battles in the 1970s – The Struggle for Recognition

Mostly, the bosses resisted the unions. They refused to give organisers access to the factory. And even if the unions had signed up large numbers of workers, the bosses refused to deal with them.

In fact, the bosses went on a big drive to organise liaison committees to try and undermine the unions. The bosses claimed that in 1978 there were over 2 600 liaison committees and 303 works committees involving over 770 000 workers. But most of these 'boots and overalls' committees were toothless and certainly did not try and represent the interests of workers in the factory.

Despite these problems, the new unions won a major breakthrough in 1974. At the Smith and Nephew plant in Pinetown, the management agreed to recognise and bargain with the National Union of Textile Workers (NUTW).

Smith and Nephew

The agreement allowed the union to elect shop stewards recognised by management. NUTW could now build a permanent and democratic organisation right on the factory floor. If the bosses wanted to kick the union out, they would have to break the agreement.

The signing of recognition agreements became an important tool for the young unions. Because it was so difficult to win increases in wages and improvements in working conditions, recognition agreements vastly improved the unions' power. They could be used as a way of encouraging workers to join and also ensured that unions could be effectively controlled by elected stewards, operating with mandates from the factory floor.

But very few bosses followed the path of Smith and Nephew. Most managements hid behind the government and said that unregistered trade unions were illegal.

In 1976, workers at the Heinemann factory, one of the Metal and Allied Workers Union's (MAWU) strongest factories on the East Rand, went on strike for recognition. The strike ended in a thumping defeat for the union.

MAWU workers show their unity at the Heinemann strike in 1975.

The Heinemann Strike

MAWU began organising at Heinemann in 1975 and resisted the bosses' attempts to install a liaison committee. Instead, they ran a campaign for recognition. The majority of workers in the plant joined the union and elected a shop stewards' committee and sent petitions to get the committee recognised.

The police and management harassed shop stewards and union members. In March 1976, the company fired twenty workers, including three shop stewards. Workers gathered outside the factory and demanded to meet with the Managing Director.

When they arrived at work the next day (Friday) the gates were locked. At the other gates the police were standing together with management. They were told that they had been fired. The workers met on the weekend and decided to go back to work on Monday.

On Monday the gates were still locked and guarded by a large group of police. Again workers demanded to see the Managing Director, but were refused. At 10 o'clock that morning they were given half an hour to leave.

As they left singing, the police attacked everyone in sight, leaving 28 workers injured.

MAWU organisers were convicted of inciting workers to strike and the union was broken in the factory. The managers would only rehire those workers who agreed to support the liaison committee. It took many months for MAWU to make up the ground it had lost during the strike.

Workers at another factory in the Transvaal, Armourplate, went on strike legally over retrenchments, in the same year. They were assisted by the UTP. Again they met with the full force of the police and ended up losing their jobs.

The government was showing where they stood in the struggle for trade unions. Right behind, and often in front of the bosses! In 1976 they began to pay more attention to the unions.

They did this in the way that they knew best: through repression and control.

6. Clamping Down – The Government and the Unions

Repression

1976 was the year of Soweto. A year in which Black students exposed the brutality of the apartheid regime and began organising themselves to challenge the power of the government.

In 1976 students rejected the government's attempts to make them learn half their subjects in Afrikaans. On 16 June, the Soweto Students Representative Council (SSRC) organised a meeting at Orlando Stadium where students could discuss the problems they were facing and make plans for the future.

As the students moved towards the stadium the police opened fire. No one really knows how many people were shot and killed on that day. But the event ignited the nation to action.

Hector Peterson was the first student killed by the police on 16 June 1976.

School boycotts and student resistance spread across the country. The apartheid regime which had stood solid since the 1960s, was rocked to its foundations.

In the events which followed June 16, the government tried to smash the resistance with bullets, batons, dogs and teargas. Hundreds of students were killed, and many thousands injured and arrested.

The government also took this opportunity to try and smash the unions. Union work was seriously disrupted by these events. Many union officials were arrested, and in November 1976, 26 officials were banned. UTP officials, the organisational leadership of MAWU and NUTW in Natal and the Transvaal, and students who worked with the WPWAB were all banned.

Although weakened by these attacks, the unions were now strong enough to survive. They had begun to build strong shop floor organisation. The government realised that they could not crush the unions by force alone. In 1976, they began to look for new ways of controlling African workers – the government called it 'reform'. For workers these reform laws meant something very different.

Labour Laws

Throughout the history of the working class in South Africa, Africans were not included in the definition of 'employee'. This divided workers as Africans could not join registered unions and were included in separate bargaining procedures.

When Africans began to organise themselves into trade unions in the 1970s, they forced the government to rethink their position. In 1977 the government passed a law which tried to extend the liaison committee system. But it was obvious that workers would not accept this.

In 1977, the government appointed the Wiehahn Commission to look into labour laws and especially the rights of African workers. It also appointed the Rieckert Commission to look at influx control laws.

The Industrial Conciliation Amendment Act 94 of 1979, the Industrial Conciliation Act 11 of 1980 and the Labour Relations Amendment Act 57 of 1981.

After these commissions gave their reports, the government was forced to make some big changes to laws controlling African workers. Three laws* were passed between 1978 and 1981, covering the recommendations of the commission.

These labour laws:

1. Gave African workers union rights and access to existing Industrial Conciliation Act bargaining structures (including industrial councils).

2. Retained the works and liaison committee systems, but allowed all races to belong to them. In this way multi-racial in-plant committees could be set up.

181

3. Allowed Blacks to do jobs formerly reserved for Whites only.

4. Retained the legal right to strike, but only if certain procedures were followed.

5. Established an industrial court.

For the first time African workers were recognised as 'employees' under industrial legislation. They now had the right to form registered trade unions. But, if they wanted to register, they had to be controlled in some way by the government.

The Industrial Court in action.

The government and bosses' attempts to stop the growth of the trade union movement were not very successful. Although some unions registered, the government was not able to kill the growing militancy of workers. In the late 1970s and early 1980s workers became even stronger. Individual unions began to build national unity within the trade union movement.

Chapter Twelve
Power in the Factories:
1979 – 1984

1979 was the year that workers joined together in a federation and formed FOSATU. After 1979, hundreds of thousands of workers were organised in different trade unions and trade union federations. By 1984 there was CUSA, SAAWU and AZACTU as well.

Some unions did not join federations at all. They remained independent. Other unions did not form federations, but in 1983 united with other organisations in the UDF.

All these unions and federations had different strengths and weaknesses, different policies and ways of organising.

But in the eyes of the bosses and government there was no difference. Together, the unions were a very serious challenge to the power and privileges of the ruling class.

This chapter discusses the struggles of these unions and union federations between 1979 and 1984.

The chapter is divided into the following sections:

1.   **The Struggle for FOSATU**

2.   **The Struggle for CUSA**

3.   **The Independent Unions**

4.   **The Struggle for SAAWU**

5.   **Black Consciousness and AZACTU**

6.   **Striking Back at TUCSA**

7.   **The Workers' Voice**

1. The Struggle for FOSATU

In 1977 a number of trade unions and co-ordinating bodies set up a committee to look into forming a new trade union federation. This committee included the ex-TUCSA affiliate, the National Union of Motor and Rubber Workers (NUMARWOSA), its 'African' parallel, the United Automobile Workers*, the TUACC and the CIWW unions*, the CCOBTU unions and the WPWAB.

But unity talks were not easy. The WPWAB argued that it was too early to form a federation. It had not yet been demanded by workers. They felt that unity formed by officials would only increase the power of the officials. They eventually withdrew from the feasibility committee.

The Food and Canning Workers Union also did not participate. The union needed to concentrate on building its own structures and was not strong enough to enter a federation.

The TUACC unions said that any new federation should be controlled by workers at all levels. They called for a tight federation which would pool resources and decide policy.

The unity talks forced a split within CCOBTU. At a meeting held in August 1978, the general secretaries of the CCOBTU unions rejected the idea of forming a new federation. But not all CCOBTU unions agreed.

The Glass and Allied Workers, Paper Wood and Allied Workers Union (PWAWU) and large sections of the Engineering and Allied Workers Union (EAWU) and the Sweet Food and Allied Workers Union (SFAWU) backed the call for unity. The last two unions eventually split from the CCOBTU affiliates.

So only two CCOBTU unions joined the Federation of South African Trade Unions (FOSATU) which was

NUMARWOSA and UAW – Soon after this NUMARWOSA and UAW merged to form the National Automobile and Allied Workers Union (NAAWU).

CIWW – The CIWW joined the TUACC unions in 1978.

185

launched in April 1979. At the launch, FOSATU claimed a membership of 45 000 with three registered and nine unregistered trade unions.

The constitution of FOSATU ensured a majority of worker delegates at all levels of decision-making in the federation. Resources would be pooled and the National Congress would make policy for the union. The central policies of the federation included:

- Non-racialism
- Worker Control
- Industrial Unions
- Shop Floor Organisation
- Worker Independence
- International Worker Solidarity
- Trade Union Unity

The first FOSATU Central Committee – 1979

By the end of 1984 FOSATU had eight affiliates and claimed to represent nearly 120 000 workers. But the federation's power was actually larger than its membership figures show. This was because many of the unions concentrated on organising in large powerful monopoly and multinational companies.

FOSATU AFFILIATES AND MEMBERSHIP – 1984

Affiliate	Membership
Chemical Workers Industrial Union – CWIU	13 750
Jewellers and Goldsmiths Union – JGU	470
Metal and Allied Workers Union – MAWU	34 000
National Automobile and Allied Workers Union – NAAWU	20 250
National Union of Textile Workers – NUTW	15 720
Paper Wood and Allied Workers Union – PWAWU	11 430
Sweet, Food and Allied Workers Union – SFAWU	12 250
Transport and General Workers Union – TGWU	11 080

One of the first issues FOSATU and other trade unions had to face in the 1980s, was the new labour laws which the government had passed. These laws led to major debates about trade union registration.

A number of unions felt that trade union registration would lead to greater controls and would not benefit workers. They said that registration would take struggle away from the workers into the hands of officials sitting on industrial councils.

FOSATU did not believe that this was necessarily the case. They saw the new laws as a site of struggle. These laws could provide some spaces where unions could win workers' rights.

FOSATU and Registration

The FOSATU unions did not register immediately. First, they said that they would register only under certain conditions. One was that they would be allowed to register as non-racial trade unions.

The government was forced to allow this, but even then, only some FOSATU unions registered and participated in industrial councils. The unions' main strategy was to use their strength on the factory floor to fight for the recognition of unions on their own terms.

But the bosses wanted unions to negotiate on the industrial councils where wages and working conditions were fixed for the whole industry. They wanted workers to negotiate through the committee system in the factory.

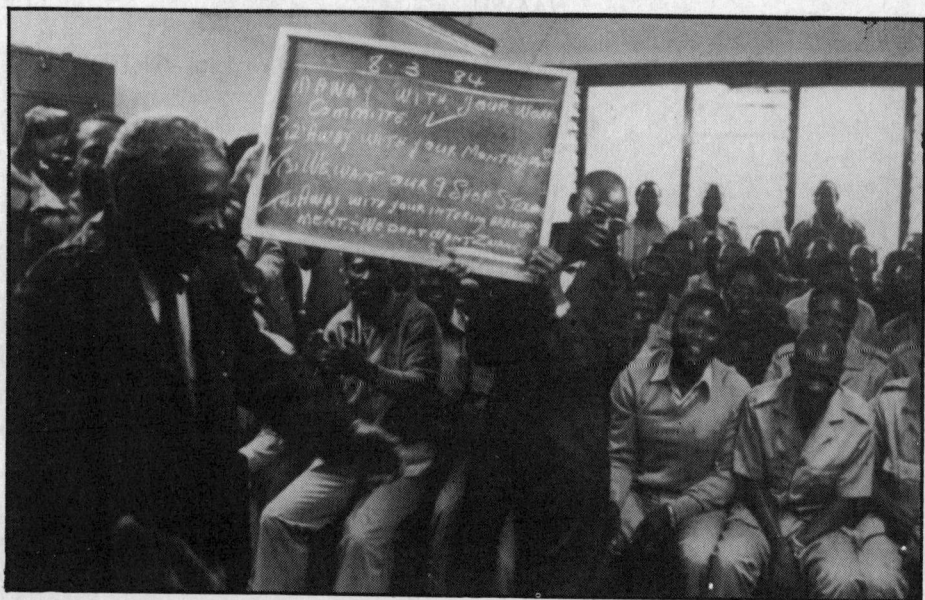

Away with works committees – Forward with shop stewards' committees!

This wasn't what workers were fighting for. They knew that their real power lay on the factory floor.
FOSATU unions wanted to use the industrial councils on their own terms. They wanted to have the

right to negotiate at plant level – where they had real control. Soon, workers saw that they would have to struggle for this.

The Struggle for Plant Level Bargaining

Volkswagen

One important way that the unions could use the industrial council and build their organisation, was to ensure that representatives acted with mandates and gave reportbacks on developments.

In 1980 motor workers at the Volkswagen (VW) plant in Uitenhage, stopped work when the magistrate of the area banned a reportback meeting from the industrial council.

3 500 workers went on strike over ten days. The police intervened and repeatedly acted against the workers with teargas and birdshot. Several workers were wounded. Workers and youth clashed with police in Uitenhage and in the townships in Port Elizabeth.

During this period NUMARWOSA and UAW grew very rapidly. Many factories organised by the unions bargained at the factory level outside the official system.

NAAWU members – May Day 1983

Other strikes among FOSATU affiliates broke out directly over the right to negotiate at the plant level.

Colgate

In 1981, Colgate management refused to negotiate wages and working conditions with the Chemical Workers Industrial Union (CWIU), unless the union joined the industrial council.

The union called for a boycott of Colgate goods and held a strike ballot. 98% of workers in the factory voted to strike. The day before the strike was to begin, Colgate recognised the union and agreed to negotiate.

East Rand Metal Industry

In 1981 and 1982 a strike wave hit the metal industry on the East Rand. In five months of 1981, there were 50 strikes involving 50 000 workers. Many of these strikes were over the right of the industrial council to fix wages in the metal industry.

Metalworkers

By 1983, MAWU had grown in strength and decided to join the industrial council. But, it set a number of conditions before it joined:

- The union reserved the right to negotiate at plant level.

- The union said that they would participate on the industrial council only if bargaining was done with shop stewards who received mandates and reported back to union members.

It was during the battles on the East Rand that workers in FOSATU began to organise a new committee to increase their power – the shop stewards' council.

FOSATU and the Shop Stewards' Council

The Germiston shop stewards' council was formed in April 1981, when there were only three unionised factories on the East Rand. At this time, metalworkers were struggling for the right to bargain at plant level.

In the council, shop stewards from different factories on the East Rand came together to discuss their common problems and ways of building their organisation.

But the council did not only stick to matters on the factory floor. One member of the Germiston shop stewards' council said:

'So the shop stewards' council has got a role to play, not only in the workplace, but in anything that affects the workers in general .....In the absence of a clear-cut organisation that does take these (workers') aspirations into effect, the shop stewards' council is going to take action.'

They did take action !

In November 1982, the East Rand Administration Board began demolishing shacks in Katlehong. By February 1983, 1 000 shacks had been demolished. The shop stewards' council felt it should provide leadership over 'community issues'.

But FOSATU's constitution did not allow for shop stewards' councils. Nevertheless, this initiative to build workers' democracy from below, soon spread to other parts of the country. Shop stewards' councils were built in all areas where FOSATU had a presence. In April 1982, FOSATU amended its constitution to formally include shop stewards' councils in the structures of the federation.

Workers discuss their problems at a shop stewards' council meeting in northern Natal.

The shop stewards' council played a very important role in developing worker leadership in FOSATU. They became the foundations of the federation and often took the lead in fighting for worker rights in and outside the factory. Soon individual industrial unions also built their own councils for their trade unions.

As a trade union federation, FOSATU grew in strength and became very powerful because of its attempt to build democracy from below – under workers' control.

But FOSATU was not the only federation of trade unions. Soon after it was formed, a number of the CCOBTU unions united to form CUSA.

2. The Struggle for CUSA

The formation of FOSATU, and the upsurge in worker militancy in the 1970s, forced the CCOBTU unions to try and consolidate their structures.

The unions which left CCOBTU to join FOSATU, accused the CCOBTU unions of not having effective decision-making structures. They said that the general secretaries of the unions had too much power.

In October 1979, CCOBTU announced that it would form a new federation. The unions lacked effective leadership and needed to build democratic decision-making structures.

In September 1980, the Council of Unions of South Africa (CUSA) was launched in Johannesburg. All the CCOBTU unions joined the federation except the Commercial, Catering and Allied Workers Union (CCAWUSA), which remained independent. At this stage, CUSA had nine affiliates with a total membership of 30 000.

By the end of 1984, CUSA had grown to over 147 000 members with twelve affiliates.

Unlike FOSATU, which was a tight federation, CUSA was a loose co-ordinating body for its affiliates. Three of its central policies were:

- Worker Control
- Industrial Unions
- Black Leadership

Some of the CUSA unions registered, but by the end of 1981 only three CUSA affiliates had joined the industrial councils. Like the FOSATU unions, they continued to push for bargaining rights outside official structures.

CUSA AFFILIATES IN 1984

Affiliate	Membership
Broom and Brush Workers Union	1 000
Building Construction and Allied Workers Union – BCAWU	27 264
Food and Beverage Workers Union – FBWU	16 124
National Union of Wine, Spirits and Allied Workers	5 000
South African Chemical Workers Union – SACWU	30 000
SA Laundry, Dry Cleaning and Dyeing Workers Union	4 771
Steel, Engineering and Allied Workers Union – SEAWU	28 927
Transport and Allied Workers Union – TAWU	23 327
Textile Workers Union (Tvl)	N/A
United African Motor and Allied Workers Union – UAMAWU	10 873
Vukani Black Guards and Allied Workers Union	514

Generally, the CUSA unions were smaller and often spread out over a large area. This made the task of organising democratically very difficult. So CUSA unions did not go on strike as often as unions from FOSATU. However, one union in CUSA was very militant. This was the National Union of Mineworkers (NUM) which CUSA launched in 1982.

War on the Mines – the NUM

Conditions and African worker rights on the mines had stayed much the same since African mineworkers went on strike in 1946. The 'induna system' was still widely used to deal with workers' problems. Low wages and the migrant labour system were still strictly enforced.

By the 1970s, workers began to show their anger.

Between 1973 and 1976 workers went on strike many times. Nearly 200 miners were killed and over 1 000 injured when they clashed with police. The miners attacked administration buildings and other symbols of the bosses' power.

Strikes broke out again in 1981 and 1982. By July 1981, 13 000 workers were out on strike. Many miners rejected a death benefit scheme implemented by the bosses. Seven miners were killed and workers damaged property at President Steyn worth R1 million.

The strikes did not die down in 1982. Over 70 000 mineworkers went on strike over wages. Again, workers were killed after they faced the power of the police.

It was under these conditions of war that the NUM was launched by CUSA in 1982. Workers joined in large numbers. They knew that they had to unite to be powerful. They also knew that NUM could give them a voice on the mines.

The National Union of Mineworkers began with ten organisers. By June 1983, the NUM claimed 20 000 members, and by the end of 1984, 110 000.

NUM did register in 1985.

NUM held its first conference in December 1982. At this conference, the union rejected registration and refused to sit on the industrial council*.

From the start, the union demanded to be accepted on workers' terms and concentrated on fighting around three main issues:

- Wages
- Health and Safety
- Job Reservation

In 1984, the mineworkers forced the Chamber of Mines to sit down and listen to their demands. 50 000 mineworkers came out on strike in protest against low wage increases. This experience strengthened the young union.

Western Deep fatal fire hit milling

Occupational health and safety drew over

By BRENDAN RYAN

WESTERN Deep Levels
during t...
fire whi...
tion by 4...
March q...

The mi...
lar for th...
workings...

The bla...
on 118 lev...
stopped m...
longwalls c...
horizon

It has bee...
a being mo...
not expect p...
affected by...
fore the end...

Six people...
Stoping te...
mining oper...
ployed to sto...
Contact Reef...

The area...
(12 000) m³ (...
(98 000 m³)...
dropped to 87...

WDL mana...
slightly to 11,...
production d...
(10 349).

While ta...
R74,356m (...

higher capital

32 000 a year are disabled at work

Compensation is call racist and a nightma

By Carolyn Dempster, Labour Reporter
Compensation for occupational disease or
injury has been condemned as racist, discriminatory and a bureaucratic nigh...
The criticisms have bee...
...the 1982 N...
...Compens...
...our resear...

Workmen's Compensation A...
"A worker...

Each year...
die and 32 00...
manent disab...
result...
ciden...
Ap...
out...
tio...
m...

Union will claim from death mine

Own Correspondent

DURBAN — The Nation-
al Union of Mineworkers
is planning to bring mas-
sive civil claims against
the Hlobane Colliery for
compensation over and
above any workmen's
compensation paid out in
respect of 68 miners who
died in a methane gas ex-
plosion in September last
year.

Mr Cyril Ramphosa,
the union's general secretary, said today that
these would total be-
tween R1 million and
R5 million and...

New Bill wi protect hea of all work

...en Dempster,

Noise levels put miners at risk of becoming deaf

By STEVEN FRIEDMAN
Labour Correspondent

DURBAN — Most miners
have a one in three chance of
impaired hearing because of...

...tion, light, n...
...or organisms
...oyees

...set out minimum standa...
only.
But be charged, evide...
at the recent inquiry into...
Hlobane mine disaster it...
cated that mine man...
ments regarded them...

Journalists yesterday had a ...te
The media people went 2,7km dow...

Gold mining ...hazar

al Diseases in Mines a
criticised the disparities
interview with
assistance for n.
and no
s trea
inimal
...ent
...el

Newspaper reports
highlight health and safety
issues taken up by NUM.

But NUM did not limit its demands to wages. It is very unsafe to work on the mines. Since 1900, about 46 000 mineworkers have died in accidents. In the 1980s, 600 mineworkers die every year from accidents. From the start, workers used their union to defend their right to health and safety.

At NUM's December conference in 1984, mineworkers targeted job reservation as the main area for struggle in 1985. The right-wing Mineworkers Union opposed NUM, but by 1986 the government was forced to scrap job reservation laws.

NUM left CUSA in December 1984. They said CUSA was not committed to unity with other unions and to worker control. This seriously weakened CUSA, which with NUM had a membership of well over 200 000.

Despite this setback, CUSA played an important role in organising workers across a number of different industries and was a force which the bosses and government could not ignore.

3. The Independent Unions

In the early 1980s, a number of trade unions which were not affiliated to any federation had a major impact on the politics of trade unions. Like the new federations, they grew in size and power.

Some of these unions were industrial unions which organised large sections of the Black working class from a particular industry. Others were general unions.

Although often smaller and regionally based, the general unions had a very big impact on union organisations.

In this period massive retrenchments and dismissals weakened some general unions. But they gained power because they united with other political organisations.

To survive, other general unions were forced to transform themselves into industrial unions.

Reviving the Food and Canning Workers Union

In 1976, the Food and Canning Workers Union (FCWU) grew stronger again in small Western Cape towns. Organisers soon found that workers at old plants remembered the union and were willing to rejoin.

In April 1979 workers at a Fattis and Monis mill in the Western Cape, were fired after urging the bosses to recognise the FCWU. Workers who went on strike in solidarity were also fired.

To resist these dismissals and increase their power, the FCWU turned to the community for support. The union launched a boycott campaign againt Fattis and Monis products and demanded the recognition of the two Food and Canning Workers Unions.

I DONT BUY FATTIS & MONIS

The boycott was a big success. Sales dropped and after seven months the workers were reinstated. One of the most important reasons why the boycott was successful was because African traders in the Cape agreed to support the boycott and not to stock Fattis and Monis products.

The Fattis and Monis boycott brought back a method of resistance that had been followed in the 1950s. For the rest of the 1980s, consumer boycotts became a powerful weapon in the hands of trade unions and other organisations of the oppressed.

Soon the union set up branches in Johannesburg and East London.

Food and canning workers were organising again!

The General Workers Union – GWU

In 1977 the Western Province General Workers Union (WPGWU) was formed from the Workers Advice Bureau. The WPGWU continued to organise workers into factory committees and fought for these structures to be recognised rather than a union.

The WPGWU opposed registration and concentrated on building strong organisation in a few plants.

Over time, the union saw the need to build a strong industry-wide presence to push workers' demands. This lesson was learnt when workers in the meat industry in the Western Cape came out on strike in 1980.

59 workers went on strike over the dismissal of fellow workers at Karoo Meat Exchange.

The company dismissed all the striking workers. They refused to deal with the union. Workers at eleven other meat firms refused to handle goods from Karoo Meat Exchange until the workers were taken back. The company soon gave in. They re-employed all the strikers.

The WPGWU managed to organise most of the workforce in the meat industry in the Western Cape, but the bosses still refused to recognise worker committees at a number of plants. In May 1980 workers at Table Bay Cold Storage and National Meat Supplies went on strike because the company refused to recognise their committee.

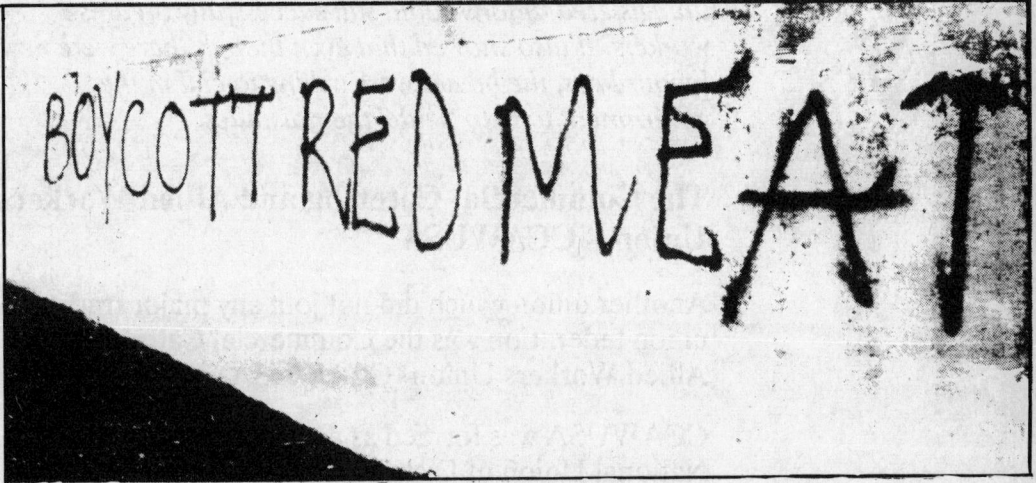

The bosses answered by firing the workers and refusing to negotiate. Almost all African workers in the industry (about 800) called a strike for a day, in support of these demands. But when the workers returned the next day, the gates were locked. They had been fired.

The union called for a boycott of red meat. Their call received widespread support, and in the first week sales dropped by 40%. But the bosses would not give in. They called in the police. Union officials were detained and by August, the union had to admit defeat. Workers had to apply to get their jobs back. Very few workers got their jobs back.

By 1979, many dockworkers in Cape Town had organised a workers' committee and demanded recognition. They were only given recognition after the workers threatened to go on strike. For the first time workers at the docks were beginning to participate in negotiations.

The early struggles of the WPGWU showed that unregistered unions could still successfully organise workers. It also showed that even though there were new labour laws, the bosses were willing to call in the government to help 'settle' their disputes.

The Commercial Catering and Allied Workers Union – CCAWUSA

Another union which did not join any major trade union federation was the Commercial Catering and Allied Workers Union (CCAWUSA).

CCAWUSA was formed as a parallel union to the National Union of Distributive Workers (NUDAW) and the National Union of Commercial and Catering Allied Workers Union (NUCCAW) in 1975. These other unions did not try and control CCAWUSA as was the case with other parallels. Also, CCAWUSA never affiliated to TUCSA.

Strikes broke out around the country in retail stores and workers organised CCAWUSA to increase their power. Between 1981 and 1984 the union membership rose from 5 000 to 33 000.

Soon the union had branches around the country and by 1985 claimed a membership of 50 000. CCAWUSA signed recognition agreements with all the major stores in the country.

The union has been active in resisting retrenchments and low wages. It is also the union which has pioneered the struggle for maternity rights for women in the country.

Trade union meeting: Women workers demand maternity rights.

MACWUSA and GWUSA

1981 and 1982 were also important years for workers in the Eastern Cape. In these years a wave of strikes swept across the area.

A number of unions emerged from these strikes. The strikes occurred at a time of mass mobilisation in the townships. In Port Elizabeth, the Port Elizabeth Black Civic Organisation (PEBCO) had mobilised thousands of township residents against conditions in the township.

From the start, workers fought for unions to take up issues in the factories and the townships.

In November 1979 workers at Ford in Port Elizabeth went on strike in protest at the dismissal of Thozamile Botha, an executive member of the community-based Port Elizabeth Black Civic Organisation (PEBCO).

The bosses at Ford met the United Automobile Workers (UAW) immediately, and agreed that Botha could return, and that workers would receive their pay for the time on strike.

Soon workers went on strike again over the racism of a

White foreman. Over the next few weeks at Ford, workers went on strike four times and the strikes spread to the nearby factories.

The UAW was unable to respond adequately to the strikes. The union negotiated wages at the industrial council but did not build solid shop floor structures at the same time.

Workers who supported PEBCO, began to argue that UAW officials were using government 'puppet' structures. They wanted to form an unregistered union which did not sit on the industrial council and addressed workers' rights in the township and the factory.

These problems led to the formation of the Motor Assembly and Components Worker Union (MACWUSA) in October 1980. The union was based at Ford, but other motor parts workers formed the General Workers Union of South Africa (GWUSA) which worked closely with MACWUSA.

This attempt to build a trade unionism which addressed workers' issues on the shop floor and in the township, gained more strength with the formation and rapid growth of SAAWU.

4. The Struggle for SAAWU

The Black Allied Workers Union (BAWU) was formed in 1972. In 1979 the South African Allied Workers Union (SAAWU) was formed when it split from BAWU and adopted a non-racial constitution.

SAAWU was an unregistered trade union. In Durban in 1979, SAAWU was transformed into a non-racial federation of trade unions. The existing 5 000 membership were divided into a number of industrial unions.

But SAAWU's strongest branch was in the Eastern Cape. This branch considered itself a general union.

The East London branch of SAAWU was opened in March 1980 with 5 000 members. By 1981, the union claimed 25 000 members.

In 1980 and 1981, strikes swept across Port Elizabeth and East London. It was during these strikes that SAAWU built its mass membership. During the strikes SAAWU signed up 60% of a factory on strike, and demanded that the bosses deal with the union.

SAAWU made some gains for its members at three factories where it negotiated a 100% pay rise with the union.

But the bosses, together with the Ciskei and South African governments, formed a united front to try and crush SAAWU. They blocked recognition, fired worker leaders and the security police harassed and detained worker and union leaders.

By July 1981, SAAWU's membership had dropped to 15 000. The bosses had defeated strikes and fired workers on a number of occasions.

SAAWU officials hold a press conference.

Despite these losses, SAAWU was strong enough to leave a mark on the politics of the Eastern Cape. SAAWU played an important role in Duncan Village near East London and especially at Mdantsane, a township in the Ciskei. Here SAAWU, or SAAWU members played the role of a community organisation. At times, union representatives and members would act off mandates given at mass meetings on issues in the townships.

In the 1980s many more unions formed and many more struggles were fought than those we have just discussed.

Some unions revived their structures and remained independent. Many new small unions emerged from strike action. Most of these unions were unregistered and some collapsed after a short while. Some affiliated to the UDF when it was formed in 1983.

Many of these unions played an important role in defending and advancing workers' political and economic rights.

Another new trade union federation was formed in August 1984. It also fought for the political and economic rights of Black workers. This fairly small federation adopted the Azanian Manifesto* and worked with AZAPO. In 1984 it affiliated to the National Forum.

Manifesto of the Azanian People – this was drawn up in opposition to the government's Constitutional Proposals in 1983, and set out the basis for a future 'democratic, anti-racist worker republic'.

5. Black Consciousness and AZACTU

BIKO AND SOLIDARITY

BLACK PEOPLE'S CONVENTION
TRIBUTE TO THE LATE
HONORARY PRESIDENT
BANTU STEPHEN BIKO
One Azania One Nation

A political organisation, the Black People's Convention (BPC), was formed in 1972. The BPC was a Black resistance organisation, which believed that Black people could only liberate themselves if they organised independently of Whites. They planned literacy campaigns, health projects, cultural activity, economic co-operatives and a general workers' union to achieve their aims.

In 1969, a number of Black students broke away from the National Union of South African Students (NUSAS) and formed the South African Students

Organisation (SASO). In 1972, SASO resolved to set up a Black Workers' Project (BWP). This project would attempt to build a Black Workers' Council, a national trade union body for all Black workers. The BWP had some successes but these were often not very permanent.

The Black Allied Workers' Union (BAWU) was also launched independently in 1972 by an executive member of the BPC. This was more of a general union, which would be serviced by the BWP.

BAWU's history was fraught with divisions. By 1984, four unions and one small federation, the National Federation of Workers (NFW), had all in some way emerged from the BAWU.

These early attempts by the Black consciousness movement at establishing trade unions, had real limits because of their lack of resources. The banning of a number of Black consciousness organisations and the detention of leaders in 1977, also severely hindered attempts to build trade unions.

It was only when AZAPO was launched in 1979 that things began to change in any major way.

The Azanian Peoples Organisation (AZAPO) was the first organisation launched after the massive clampdown in 1977. Unlike earlier Black consciousness organisations, AZAPO placed far more emphasis on organising Black workers.

The formation of AZAPO, and the massive increase in trade unionism in the late 1970s, led to a number of unions being formed. They openly supported a Black consciousness ideology. The unions often grew from labour clinics set up by AZAPO.

By February 1984 the Black consciousness unions began holding talks. They issued a declaration of intent in May.

Some issues agreed upon by these unions in February 1984 were:

- the importance of the unity of Black workers in the struggle against all forms of oppression, exploitation and discrimination

- the right of all workers to organise into structures which defend their interests

- the need to co-ordinate resources

- the need for joint action on common issues of concern

- the need to encourage a spirit of solidarity and unity within the Black working class and Black community

- the need to promote, develop and maintain authentic Black working class leadership

The unions who issued the declaration, united in the Azanian Confederation of Trade Unions (AZACTU) in August 1984.

The largest AZACTU unions were the Black Allied Mining and Construction Workers Union (BAMCWU), and the Insurance and Assurance Workers Union of SA (IAWUSA), which each claimed a membership of over 30 000 out of the total AZACTU membership of around 75 000.

Both these unions were involved in major disputes in 1983 and 1984.

In 1983, the IAWUSA went on strike at Liberty Life and picketed the company for the recognition of their union.

At Penge Asbestos Mine in the Northern Transvaal, 1 700 workers went on a three week strike. The workers demanded a minimum wage of R10 a shift and the recognition of BAMCWU. The strikers were all dismissed, evicted from their hostels and sent back to the bantustans.

asbestosis – a killer disease which people can get from working with asbestos.

BAMCWU also demanded that evicted workers be examined by a doctor for asbestosis*. The issue was taken to court, but the court said that the workers were fired and did not have to be examined.

After this, BAMCWU began a campaign to have the asbestos mining industry closed down.

Other unions in AZACTU included:

- African Allied Workers Union – AAWU
- Amalgamated Black Workers Union – ABWU
- Black Electronics and Electrical Workers Union – BEEWU
- Black General Workers Union – BLAGWU
- Hotel, Liquor, Catering and Allied Workers Union – HOTELICA
- National Union of Workers of SA – NUWSA

The growth of unions in the 1980s directly challenged the system of exploitation and oppression. At the same time these unions seized power from the once numerically powerful TUCSA.

6. Striking Back at TUCSA

At first the new labour laws helped the TUCSA unions. They were willing to use all aspects of the law, even if it did not directly advance workers' interests. By 1983, TUCSA reached a high point in its membership. There were 57 affiliated trade unions claiming to represent over 500 000 workers.

But after this date, the membership dropped rapidly. By 1986, there were only 150 000 members remaining in TUCSA, and a decision was taken to disband the federation.

Any growth in TUCSA's membership was not because they mobilised around issues which affected African workers. TUCSA organised to get benefits for its members, but it did not fight for factory rights.

In the early 1980s, TUCSA openly opposed the new democratic unions. They called for greater controls over these unions. They said unregistered trade unions must be banned. They also asked companies to deny the newer unions' stop orders.

These unions used the privilege of the 'closed shop' to resist the advance of the more militant unions. Supported by the law, the TUCSA unions could get a membership without workers even having a choice in the issue.

But the newer unions began to challenge this. They organised workers in factories even where TUCSA unions had membership. Workers joined the unions and were prepared to strike to force the bosses to recognise them.

Soon, TUCSA found that it had been beaten.

We can see that the early 1980s were important years for trade unions in South Africa. African workers organised in mass organisations to defend and advance their interests inside and outside the factory.

By 1984, many gains had been made.

Workers Unite – MAWU Annual General Meeting

7. The Workers' Voice

Despite massive attempts by the government and bosses to resist, workers had built their trade unions into a powerful force in South Africa.

In earlier years, African workers had struggled for their unions to survive. They had made very few gains. But, by the 1980s, African workers found a voice – they began to take control of their own lives.

Workers demanded:

- the right to strike
- the right to safe and healthy working conditions
- the right to have a say over retrenchments
- the right to have access to company information
- the right to protection from hazards to pregnancy
- the right to attend clinics before and after pregnancy
- the right to control pension contributions*
- an end to sexual harassment
- maternity rights and child care facilities
- equal pay for equal work
- May Day, June 16 and March 21 as paid public holidays
- an end to apartheid
- troops out of the townships
- one person, one vote.

pension strikes – in 1981 there were about 27 pension strikes involving 30 000 workers. Unions from all different federations, independent unions as well as un-unionised workers opposed and defeated an attempt by the government to pass a law which would give the bosses greater control of their pension money.

These were some of the issues which workers fought for in the late 1970s and early 1980s.

These are still some of the issues which workers in trade unions are fighting today.

Hayibo! Workers have grown strong in their trade unions. But they still have a very long way to go.

By 1984, trade unions had only organised a small percentage of the working class. Trade unions were still divided. Trade union struggles were also often divided from struggles in the townships.

But trade unions do not exist independently of each other. An injury to one is an injury to all! Throughout the first five years of the 1980s most of the large trade unions were involved in unity talks.

Nor did any of the trade unions exist independently of township struggles. It was their members who lived in the townships.

Chapter Thirteen
The Struggle for Unity

By 1983, the economy in South Africa was in the middle of a recession. Unemployment and prices were rising. The government in South Africa was also becoming increasingly isolated.

Throughout South Africa, the masses mobilised and organised against the apartheid regime.

By the early 1980s, trade unions began defending and advancing workers' demands inside and outside the factory.

But to do this, trade unions were forced to build unity in two ways:

- with organisations outside the factory
- amongst trade unions themselves.

This chapter looks at these struggles between 1980 and 1985.

The chapter is divided into the following sections:

1. **The 1980s – The Search for Unity**

2. **Trade Unions and Political Unity**

3. **The Stayaway Campaigns**

4. **Consumer Boycotts – Industry and Government: Two Sides of the Same Bloody Coin**

5. **The Struggle for Trade Union Unity**

1. The 1980s – The Search for Unity

In the early 1980s apartheid South Africa began to collapse. Trade unions, and community organisations had grown in strength and power.

Inflation, retrenchments and rising unemployment, low wages, no infrastructure in townships and bantustans, the collapse of bantu education, and rising rents were some of the issues the workers had to confront.

At the same time, the government's attempt to impose its new political constitution on Blacks only fueled mass resistance.

Once again, the government answered in the way they knew best – repression.

The early 1980s did not only see the growth of organisation in the factories; workers and the oppressed were active in organising and mobilising where they lived – in the townships.

Youth congresses, women's groups and civic associations grew up all around South Africa in the small towns and the large cities. Organised under the banner of the Congress of South African Students (COSAS), students took the struggle forward in the fight to build democratic Student Representative Councils (SRCs). A large network of organisations was built up over this time.

With the government attempting to launch its new political constitution, the need for a united response from the oppressed became more urgent.

The National Forum (NF)

In June 1983, a number of political organisations and trade unions came together to launch the National Forum (NF). Both CUSA and AZACTU affiliated to the Forum which included AZAPO, the Azanian

Students Movement (AZASM), Azanian Youth Organisation (AZAYO) and the Cape Action League (CAL). SAAWU and the Congress of South African Students (COSAS) sent observers to the first meeting of the NF, but then withdrew. All in all, there were 800 delegates from over 200 organisations represented.

By December 1984 four meetings of the NF had been held. In July 1984 the 'Manifesto of the Azanian People' was formally adopted.

The NF was built as a loose structure. It was seen as a forum for discussion and debate, where a whole range of issues could be discussed. The Forum was meant to provide minimum programmes by consensus for local organisations to take up. So, the Forum did not try to initiate any major national campaigns.

Two months after the formation of the National Forum, the UDF was launched in Cape Town. A number of organisations came together to unite in different local struggles against the government.

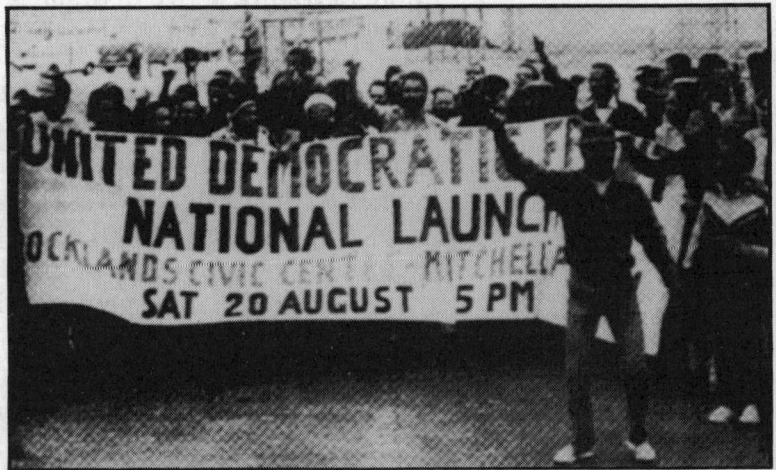

Supporters celebrate the launch of the United Democratic Front on 20 August 1983.

The United Democratic Front (UDF)

By its first conference in December 1983, the UDF claimed to represent over 560 affiliates.

The UDF was to be loosely organised with regional co-operation, although a number of UDF regions set up UDF area committees. The major policy statement of the Front, was the UDF Declaration which commits affiliates to unite 'all our people wherever they may be...to fight for freedom.'

The highest decision-making body was the General Council. Each affiliate would be represented in the General Council by two delegates. Affiliates were given independence so long as their actions did not go against the aims of the UDF Declaration.

A number of unions joined the UDF when it was formed in 1983. CUSA, participated in both the UDF and NF.

Both the UDF and NF accepted the principle of working class leadership in struggles against oppression and exploitation. They repeatedly called on trade unions to affiliate and join their ranks.

But, FOSATU and a number of larger independent unions refused to affiliate to either organisation. In the 1980s, workers and trade unions actively helped shape struggles outside the factory.

The difficult question of an alliance between trade unions and organisations in townships was on the agenda.

2. Trade Unions and Political Unity

The unions which didn't affiliate to the UDF and NF were willing to co-operate in joint campaigns. These unions also encouraged their members to participate in township based organisations.

Some trade unions were wary of how strong trade unions would be if they affiliated to either of these organisations. In the UDF, each organisation was only given two delegates. This would give small organisations the same decision making power over policy matters as a mass based trade union.

The fact that many trade unions did not affiliate to the UDF, did not mean that unions did not participate in politics. What it did mean however, was that at times trade unions took up political issues independently of other organisations.

FOSATU workers reject the new constitution.

Trade Unions – Tackling the Issues

Although FOSATU did not affiliate to the UDF, it actively opposed the government's new constitution.

NAAWU members in the Eastern Cape walked door to door, urging workers and others not to vote at the time of the government's new constitution. Other unions in the Western Cape openly challenged Labour Party leaders.

Trade unions called for a no vote in the referendum and challenged their bosses to take a position on basic human rights. The unions put forward the idea of one person one vote.

MAWU asked the bosses to sign a petition rejecting the proposed Koornhof Bills.

But soon it became clear that trade unions could not afford to continue to take up issues on their own. They had still organised only a small percentage of the working class.

Workers in trade unions were also active in struggles which blew up in the townships. From November 1984, a number of stayaways were called. This made the question of an alliance between trade unions and organisations in the townships even more urgent.

3. The Stayaway Campaigns

November 1984

In August 1984, youth and student groups on the East Rand gave support to a consumer boycott called by the SFAWU.

By September 1984, rent boycotts broke out in different townships around the Transvaal. Bloody violence and conflict followed, as the police and army moved into the townships. War was declared.

Students now turned to the trade union movement for support. The result was the November 1984 stayaway.

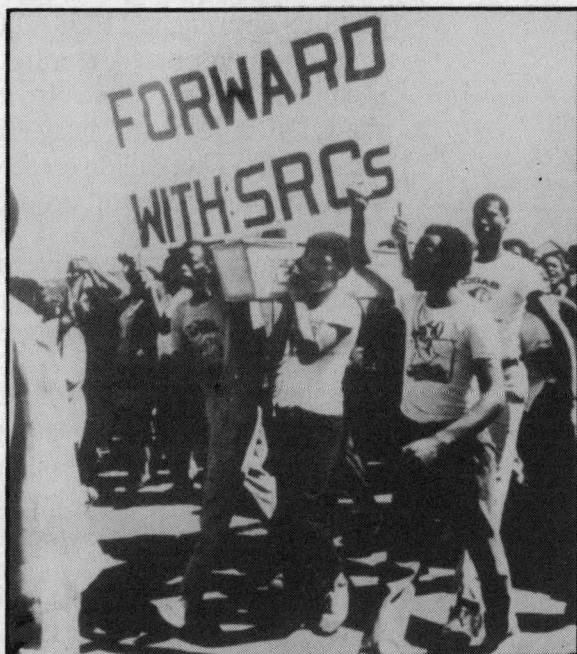

Students make their demands heard.

Students organised under COSAS also had many other grievances. They had had enough of 30 years of bantu education and demanded that their voice be heard. They urged their parents to listen to their demands.

A stayaway called by COSAS in October 1984, received some support from trade unions in the Transvaal. This encouraged students to call another stayaway over a wide range of student and township demands.

Demands of the COSAS Transvaal Region – November 1984:

- Student Representative Councils (SRCs) in every school

- an end to all age restrictions

- the reinstatement of every single expelled student

- free books and schooling

- an end to all corporal punishment

- protest against the new constitution which excludes the majority of people and which is racist and anti-worker.

COSAS approached FOSATU, the UDF and other unions for support. A committee was formed which included representatives from FOSATU, GAWU and the UDF. A joint stayaway was called for 5 and 6 November. This call also received support from CUSA and other independent unions.

The stayaway was a massive success and it was estimated that over 800 000 workers stayed away from work and 400 000 students boycotted classes.

The stayaway was not without its problems for the trade unions. At the parastatal, SASOL, the bosses fired 5 500 CWIU workers. Supervised by the police and army, workers were bussed back to the bantustans after supporting the stayaway call.

It took many negotiations, and threats of national solidarity action by unity unions, before the SASOL management agreed to reinstate the workers.

The stayaway was followed by police action. Student activists, the FOSATU president and officials from MAWU, NUTW, CUSA and TGWU were detained.

The demands made in the stayaway were not achieved. But the action showed that if they are united, workers in trade unions in alliance with other organisations could have a powerful impact on the economic and political development of the nation.

But in March 1985 events in the Eastern Cape did not run as smoothly.

March 1985

In March 1985, PEBCO, and the Port Elizabeth Women's Organisation (PEWO) jointly called a stayaway in Port Elizabeth. The call was supported by other UDF affiliated community organisations and trade unions, including MACWUSA. There was to be a consumer boycott on March 16 to 18, and a stayaway on March 18.

The demands for the stayaway focussed on massive retrenchments, the price increase of petrol and paraffin and the increase in General Sales Tax. A few days before the stayaway, FOSATU, CUSA, GWU, FCWU, CCAWUSA, the Domestic Workers Association of South Africa (DWASA), AZAPO and the Azanian Students Movement (AZASM) issued a joint statement disassociating themselves from the call.

These organisations claimed that:

- at this stage, workers did not support the call
- the call did not express worker interests – some demands were seen as national issues which couldn't be solved by a local stayaway
- workers had not participated in the decision to call a stayaway
- the call was divisive, because it ignored Coloured workers in the area.

Despite this statement, in terms of numbers, the stayaway was a massive success with almost 100% support in the area. The divisions which emerged however, did little to help build unity in the area.

Funeral for fourteen Langa victims held in Port Elizabeth during March 1985.

At the time of the Langa shooting on 21 March, there were many divisions between some trade unions and other organisations in the area. But they were partly smoothed over in the Eastern Cape by May 1985.

In May, FOSATU met with representatives from the Uitenhage branches of COSAS, AZASO, MACWUSA, the Uitenhage Youth Congress, the Uitenhage Women's Organisation and a church ministers' organisation to resolve their differences.

The organisations agreed to co-operate in future, to stop public attacks on organisations, and to prevent physical violence between members of the different organisations.

4. Consumer Boycotts – Industry and Government: Two Sides of the Same Bloody Coin

By the middle of 1985, consumer boycotts spread across the country. These boycotts forged unity between trade unions and political organisations. Resistance against the bosses and the government was growing.

In July 1985, the government imposed a state of emergency in a number of magisterial districts around the land. The government and bosses were on the attack. Retrenchments increased the ranks of the unemployed, and the police and army had occupied the townships.

In the past, consumer boycotts had been used to mobilise the community around a particular industrial dispute. Boycotts focussed on one employer or product. The consumer boycotts which swept over the country in 1985 made national political demands.

In most areas, the consumer boycott was initiated by the UDF or affiliated organisations. It began in a number of small towns in the Cape, but soon spread to the Eastern Cape and in August 1985 to the rest of the country.

In Pietermaritzburg, a consumer boycott initiated by the FOSATU shop stewards' council demanded the reinstatement of dismissed workers from Sarmcol. CCAWUSA, GWU, COSAS and other UDF affiliates, the Natal Indian Congress (NIC), the National Education Union of South Africa (NEUSA), AZASM, and the African Peoples Democratic Union of South Africa (APDUSA), all gave their support for the call. Some organisations however, felt that national demands should have been included in the call for a consumer boycott.

At times national demands were mixed with local

issues. But, in all centres trade unions gave their support to the campaign.

In August 1985 FOSATU, together with the GWU, FCWU, NUM, CCAWUSA and the CTMWA agreed to launch a national consumer boycott of White shops.

A national co-ordinating committee was appointed to organise and monitor the boycott.

The demands said:
- Lift the State of Emergency
- Remove the army and police from the townships
- Release all detainees
- Give full political rights to all.

This consumer boycott was not as successful as some of the boycotts called in smaller towns and never fully got off the ground.

But through the boycotts, a far larger basis for unity now existed between trade unions and township based organisations.

At the same time as these battles were being fought in the townships and strikes were breaking out throughout the country, trade unions were also involved in unity talks.

5. The Struggle for Trade Union Unity

Unity Talks

Langa – August 1981

In August 1981, a number of trade unions met in Langa in the Cape and took four resolutions:
- on industrial councils
- the Ciskei
- bannings and detentions

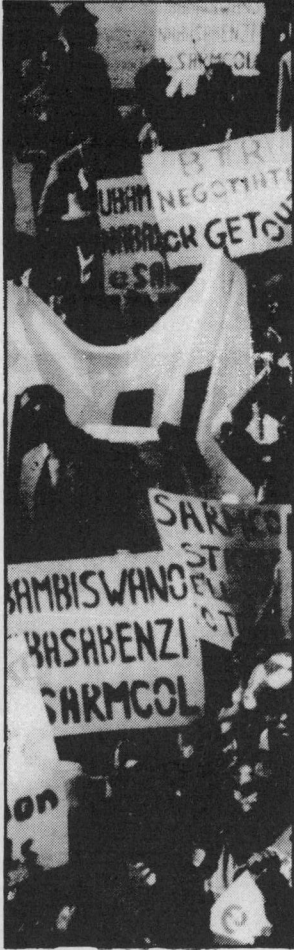

Call for a consumer boycott to support the Sarmcol workers on strike

- and solidarity action.

The meeting resolved that regional special solidarity committees should be established throughout the country to initiate solidarity action between the different trade unions.

Unions present at the Conference of Trade Unions in Langa – August 1981

- The General Workers Union – GWU
- The Food and Canning Workers Union and African Food and Canning Workers Union – FCWU/AFCWU
- The Federation of South African Trade Unions – FOSATU
- Council of Unions of South Africa – CUSA
- South African Allied Workers Union – SAAWU
- Motor Assembly and Components Workers Union of South Africa – MACWUSA
- The General Workers Union of South Africa – GWUSA
- The Black Municipal Workers Union – BMWU
- Commercial, Catering and Allied Workers Union – CCAWUSA
- The Orange Vaal General Workers Union – OVGWU
- General and Allied Workers Union – GAWU
- Cape Town Municipal Workers Association – CTMWA

It was the death of an African Food and Canning Workers Union official, Neil Aggett, which sparked off the first solidarity action.

Neil Aggett was found dead in police cells at John Vorster Square on 5 February 1982. Police said that he had hung himself.

The regional solidarity action committees in the Transvaal were used to organise a period of protest on 11 February.

The call was made by the AFCWU and FOSATU. It is reported that about 100 000 workers were involved in solidarity action around the country.

223

The work stoppage broke tension between them. For the first time, the registered and unregistered unions acted together.

FOSATU's Stand

Two weeks before a unity meeting called for April 1982, FOSATU held its second National Conference.

The meeting adopted a speech made by the general secretary, Joe Foster, as policy. In the speech, FOSATU's position on trade union unity was laid down.

The speech opposed 'ad-hoc unity' as displayed by the Aggett stoppage. The way forward was to build 'disciplined unity' on the basis of unions participating jointly in a 'tight federation'. Decisions had to be taken in consultation and backed by worker mandates.

The structure of FOSATU was put forward as an example of a tight federation with disciplined unity.

Unity talks in Cape Town

Langa – April 1982

There was much debate at the second unity meeting held at Langa. Unions outside FOSATU objected that participation in a structure as proposed by FOSATU would allow FOSATU to dominate.

MACWUSA and GWUSA stormed out of the meeting. They opposed registration and participation in industrial councils. But other unions did not feel that these issues obstructed the moves to unity.

By the time of the next meeting in Port Elizabeth, MACWUSA and GWUSA had united with other unions to present seven non-negotiable principles for unity.

Port Elizabeth – July 1982

At the Port Elizabeth meeting, seven non-negotiable principles were spelt out by SAAWU, MACWUSA, GWUSA, MGWUSA, GAWU and OVGWU, and a new union, the South African Transport Workers Union (SATWU).

These principles were:

- non-registration
- factory floor bargaining
- federation policy to be built on affiliates
- worker control of unions
- non-racialism
- participation in community politics
- the rejection of 'reactionary bodies' in South Africa and overseas.

At these talks, the unregistered GWU moved closer to FOSATU and other registered industrial unions. It resolved to stop organising in four key industries where FOSATU unions had members.

After this meeting, the GWU urged all the unions to

meet again in April 1983 to discuss the practical steps towards forming a new federation.

Athlone – March 1983

At this meeting, all the unions involved in the unity talks (except for CUSA) were represented by large shop steward delegations.

Although unity was seen as essential, the unions were divided on how to form unity. The seven principles presented at the previous talks were rejected.

Some of the newer unions argued that regional committees should be established in mass worker meetings. Not enough workers were organised to form a federation.

FOSATU and other independent unions said that the regional committees had already failed. Building a trade union federation would be far more democratic.

The meeting set up a committee to study the practical steps needed to form a federation. Unions which did not wish to form a federation were asked not to join the feasibility committee.

June to October 1983

There was still some tension between different groups of unions and federations. Some unions accused SAAWU of attempting to recruit GWU and FOSATU members in Durban.

At a meeting in June, all the unions were supposed to provide concrete information on membership and areas of organising. SAAWU, MACWUSA, GAWU and CUSA didn't provide information which showed proof of their claims. They argued that their word should be trusted.

CUSA still participated in talks, but opposed the other unions on the question of non-racialism and were wary of Whites in leadership positions in the trade union movement.

FOSATU and other independent unions said that the other unions weren't serious about unity. They felt they were strong enough to go ahead.

March 1984

The next round of talks took place in March 1984. FOSATU and other unions suggested that the general unions could join the federation at a later stage, when they were ready and were industrially based. These unions would be given observer status, or could withdraw from the talks if they wished.

SAAWU, GAWU, MACWUSA, GWUSA and MGWU walked out of the talks. They accused the others of expelling them. All these unions had affiliated to the United Democratic Front after its launch in August 1983.

CUSA, FOSATU, GWU, CTMWA, FCWU and CCAWUSA resolved at the meeting to form a sub-committee to draft a constitution for the new federation. Together these unions represented well over 300 000 workers in the major sectors of the South African economy.

In 1984, the need for unity became more urgent. The police and army had moved into the townships, which had become war zones. The need to resist these moves forced the trade unions into closer unity with each other, and with organisations in the townships.

FOSATU and other unions also worked closely together to organise May Day rallies in the Transvaal in 1985.

A meeting was scheduled for June 1985. This meeting was to approve the draft constitution, and arrange a date for the launch of the federation. FOSATU urged the feasibility committee to invite all progressive trade unions, including the newly formed Azanian Confederation of Trade Unions (AZACTU).

1985 May Day Rally

June 1985 – All In Conference

The National Executive Committees of 23 trade unions attended the meeting. But there were still disagreements.

Many unions felt that they had not been included in drawing up the constitution and were badly treated by unions who had remained in the feasibility committee. At the meeting, AZACTU objected to the non-racialism of the unions in the feasibility committee and no longer participated in moves to unity.

By August 1985, CUSA also withdrew. CUSA was committed to Black leadership and supported AZACTU's view. Their affiliates had also come into conflict with some of FOSATU's unions.

CUSA's largest affiliate, NUM remained in the talks.

SA Trade Union
Co-ordinating Bodies
in 1985

	Membership
COSATU	565 000
CUSA	180 000
AZACTU	86 851
TUCSA	360 000
SACL	100 000

NUM had disaffiliated from CUSA in December 1984 and committed itself to unity.

August to November 1985 – The Formation of COSATU

The unions in the feasibility committee, together with NUM and unions affiliated to the UDF, met in August 1985 and set the date for the launch of the 'superfederation'. In November, four years after the first talks were held, the Congress of South African Trade Unions (COSATU) was launched in Durban.

Claiming a membership of over 500 000, COSATU was the largest trade union in the history of the South African working class.

Thirty-three trade unions from all sectors of the economy attended the inaugural congress of COSATU.

Following the policy of 'one union one industry', these unions were urged to merge and form twelve industrial trade unions.

Workers celebrate at the inaugural congress of COSATU in December 1985.

229

**Paid-up Membership of Affiliated Trade Unions at the
Inaugural Congress of COSATU – November 1985**

AFFILIATE	MEMBERSHIP
Amalgamated Black Workers Union (ABWU)	1 000
Brick, Clay and Allied Workers Union (BCAWU)	748
Commercial, Catering and Allied Workers Union (CCAWUSA)	50 345
Commercial Distributive Workers Union (CDWU)	1 600
Cleaning Services and Allied Workers Union (CSAWU)	850
Cape Town Municipal Workers Association (CTMWA)	11 097
Chemical Workers Industrial Union (CWIU)	20 700
Food and Canning Workers Union (FCWU)	26 455
General and Allied Workers Union (GAWU)	19 076
General Workers Union (GWU)	20 000
General Workers Union of South Africa (GWUSA)	2 905
Health and Allied Workers Union (HAWU)	1 111
Metal and Allied Workers Union (MAWU)	36 789
Motor Assembly and Component Workers Union of South Africa (MACWUSA)	3 100
Municipal Workers Union of South Africa (MWUSA)	9 249
National Automobile and Allied Workers Union (NAAWU)	20 338
National General Workers Union (NGWU) and Retail and Allied Workers Union (RAWU)	6 037
National Iron, Steel, Metal Workers Union (NISMAWU)	976
National Post Office and Allied Workers Union (NAPAWU)	2 163
National Union of Textile Workers (NUTW)	23 241
National Union of Mineworkers (NUM)	100 000
Paper Wood and Allied Workers Union (PWAWU)	11 856
Retail and Allied Workers Union (RAWU) Cape Town	3 830
South African Allied Workers Union (SAAWU)	25 032
South African Domestic Workers Association (SADWA)	4 500
South African Mineworkers Union (SAMWU)	3 029
South African Railways and Harbour Workers Union (SARWHU)	8 220
South African Scooter Transport and Allied Workers Union (SASTAWU)	4 700
South African Textile and Allied Workers Union (SATAWU)	1 900
Sweet, Food and Allied Workers Union (SFAWU)	19 596
South African Tin Workers Union (SATWU)	581
Transport and General Workers Union (TGWU)	11 000
United Mining, Metal and Allied Workers of South Africa (UMMAWOSA)	8 335

COSATU was formed as a democratically structured federation of trade unions. It supported the policy of 'one union one industry' and strongly urged affiliates to merge as soon as possible. COSATU also stated that one of its priorities would be to organise farmworkers and the unemployed.

The new federation endorsed the policies of non-racialism and worker control. It also actively committed the federation to take up campaigns to defend and advance the political and economic demands of the working class.

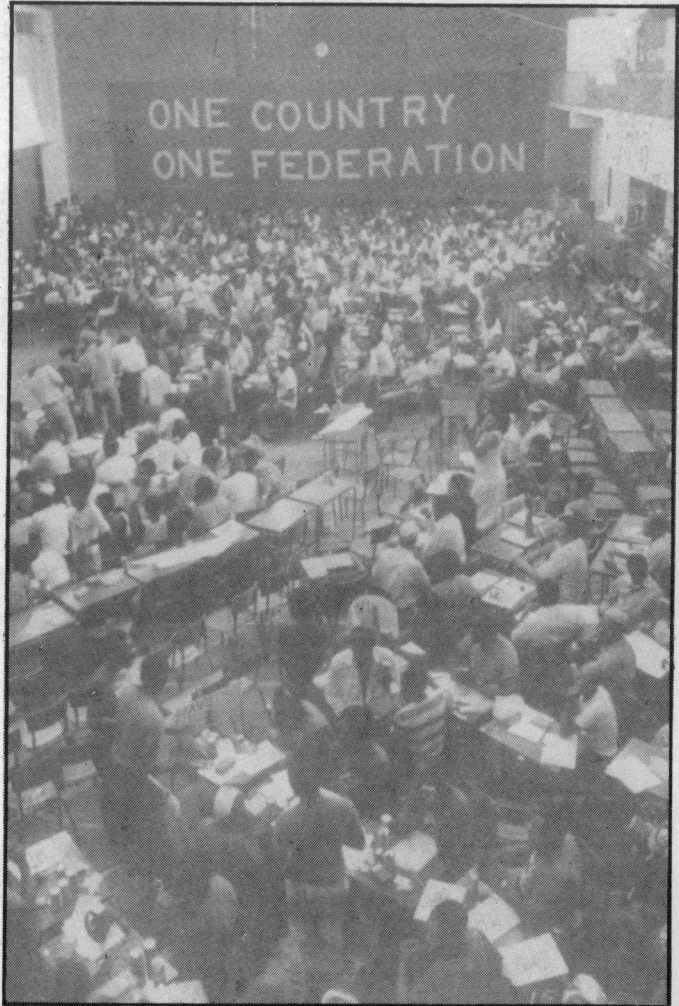

Delegates discuss policy at the inaugural congress of COSATU.

The Inaugural Congress resolved that COSATU should not affiliate to any political organisations, but should take up 'political struggles through the membership and structures at local, regional and national levels, as well as through disciplined alliances with progressive community and political organisations, whose interests are compatible with the interests of the workers and whose organisational practices further the interests of the working class.'

The formation of COSATU was a giant step forward for the trade union movement and the working class in South Africa. With over 500 000 paid-up members it was bound to have a major impact on the political and economic struggles unfolding in our nation.

Chapter Fourteen
Apartheid in Crisis: 1984 –1988

In the previous chapter we talked about the search for trade union unity in the 1980s. The struggle for unity took place at a time when both the bosses, the government and the working class were facing many problems. The economic and political problems faced by capitalism and apartheid were so serious that they could not simply be solved by old apartheid tactics. Every attempt by the bosses and the government to solve them led to more resistance. When economic and political problems are so serious, we say that the capitalist and apartheid system is in a crisis.

In this chapter we will discuss the economic and political crisis of apartheid in the 1980s.

The chapter is divided into the following sections:

1. **The Economic Crisis**

2. **The Political Crisis**

3. **The Bosses and Government Fight Back**

The crisis that South Africa experienced in the 1980s was experienced by all the capitalist countries in the world. We must remember that the many factors that make up a crisis are not easy to separate in real life. The different parts of the crisis influence each other all the time. To help explain the crisis, we however have to discuss each factor in turn.

1. The Economic Crisis

The Fiscal Crisis

When a government's expenditure is permanently above its income, we say that there is a fiscal crisis. In South Africa, to run the apartheid system and subsidise the capitalists, the government needs a lot of money. The government can get this money in a number of ways. It taxes individuals, the companies and the mines. The government also charges General Sales Tax, which hits hard into the workers' pockets. Because of rising government expenditure on the army, police, the salaries of Members of Parliament and other senior civil servants, the bantustans and the entire apartheid system, the government is unable to find enough money. The mining, farming and manufacturing bosses are resisting paying further taxes on their money. This has made the government desperate. They have tried to solve this problem by printing more money, but this only adds to inflation*.

inflation – this is a general rise in the price of goods and services. Where there was a general fall in prices it would be called deflation. The rise in prices is measured by the Consumer Price Index published by the government.

Inflation

When the prices of goods keep rising we say there is inflation. We saw that the government's attempt to solve its fiscal crisis leads to inflation. Another factor that adds to inflation is that South Africa imports inflation. When there is inflation in Europe and America, it leads to a rise in prices in South Africa. This happens because South Africa has to import most of the machinery it needs for economic growth. So when the prices of these machines go up, there is an increase in the price of the goods produced by these machines. Another factor that adds to inflation is that many important goods in South Africa are produced by the big monopoly companies and the government. These companies and the government contribute to inflation by raising the prices of the goods they produce. They increase prices as a way of making sure that their profits remain high.

Unemployment

To keep profits high and workers' wages low, all capitalist countries rely on a pool of unemployed workers. Since the 1960s the bosses have been using more machinery in production. This has meant that more workers have been retrenched and are unemployed. New workers looking for jobs can no longer find work as they have been replaced by machines. This leads to what is called **structural unemployment.**

Groups of unemployed workers can be seen in front of many factories in South Africa.

fiscal – the word fiscal comes from the Latin word **fiscus**. It refers to the income that the state gets from the public and how it expends this income. So a fiscal crisis is a crisis where expenditure of the state is far greater than its income, and the State cannot correct this by normal means.

foreign exchange – this is all foreign currency. Some foreign currency is more widely used in trade, tourism and other international transactions. It is easier to exchange these currencies so they are referred to as convertible. The most important convertible currency is the US dollar. Other important currencies are the Pound Sterling (United Kingdom), Deutschemark (Germany), Swiss Franc, Yen (Japan), and the French Franc. Many currencies are not convertible because they are in short supply and unstable. The currencies of Socialist countries are not convertible because the way in which they trade with each other and the rest of the world is different.

As inflation rose and the government battled with its fiscal* crisis, the bosses lost confidence in the government. The bosses showed this by not building new factories or expanding existing ones. This fall in investment helped to boost the already high numbers of the unemployed.

Balance of Payments Problems

In order to buy the machines needed for production, South Africa has to borrow money from the countries selling these machines. Only after South Africa has this foreign money known as foreign exchange*, can it buy these machines and the other goods it needs to grow.

In the mid-1980s South Africa experienced a balance of payments problem. This means that it could not get enough foreign money to buy the goods necessary for its growth. There were a number of factors that contributed to this problem:

- Foreign companies are an important source of foreign exchange. One of the ways in which they help bring in foreign exchange is when they use their international connections for exporting their goods. When many of these companies left South Africa in the mid-1980s as a result of the crisis, South Africa lost an important source of foreign exchange.

- The political crisis also led to another problem. Under pressure from anti-apartheid groups, many overseas banks refused to lend money to South Africa. But the most important reason for their refusal was that they were not sure if South Africa could repay this money. Like the bosses inside South Africa, they had also lost confidence in the government.

- In the past, South Africa had borrowed money from the International Monetary Fund (IMF) and foreign banks. This money had to be paid back in foreign exchange. As less and less capital flowed into the country, South Africa had to use its foreign exchange reserves to repay its loans to these banks. In 1985, South Africa's reserves were so low that it stopped repayment of all foreign loans.

value of the rand – how much foreign currency you need to buy a rand. For instance, during the 1984 – 1985 crisis you needed more than R2.00 to buy one American dollar.

The shortage of foreign exchange and the low value of the rand* have combined to block the possibility of a quick solution to the economic crisis. Instead, the balance of payments problem has made the crisis worse. With no foreign exchange to buy machines and other imports, the South African economy was limited in how fast it could grow. The weak rand also made imports very expensive.

All these factors combined to plunge South Africa into one of its deepest economic crises. It was also a time in which the nation was hit by the biggest strike wave in its history. This strike wave must also be seen as part of the general struggle against apartheid and capitalism. Although the strikes began as demands for higher wages, they were soon linked with the struggles in the community. They became a part of the mass resistance which contributed to the general political crisis for the government.

2. The Political Crisis

School Boycotts

Between 1984 and 1986 thousands of students boycotted school in protest against 'gutter education'. They said that they are not struggling for the same education as that given to White students. They adopted the slogan of 'People's education for people's power'. In this period the students also forged alliances with community organisations and trade unions. This alliance first found expression in the formation of the Soweto Parents Crisis Committee (SPCC). Further national developments led to the formation of the National Education Crisis Committee (NECC), which addressed the education crisis on a national scale. It involved community organisations and trade unions as well as student and youth organisations. These struggles sparked off many other community struggles.

Rent Boycotts

From the close of 1984, South Africa became a battleground for the political control of the townships. On the one side was the working class and its allies in the townships – mainly the students and youth. On the other side was the government and its allies, the vigilantes and local authorities. The rising cost of living and especially rent increases led to mass resistance and a boycott of rents.

As the crisis deepened many communities boycotted rent.

The rent boycott became a very serious issue for the government because the local authorities depended on rents to finance themselves.

Consumer Boycotts

As the communities came under increasing attack, workers resorted to consumer boycotts to try and make their grievances heard. These boycotts were directed at all White businesses. Organisations used the boycott as a political weapon to force the government to give in to the community's demands. Although demands differed from area to area, most of the areas demanded the removal of troops from the townships and the granting of political rights to all.

The Struggle against the Black Local Authorities

The most bitter struggles in this period were waged against the political structures of apartheid and especially the Black Local Authorities. In 1976, the Bantu Affairs Administration Boards became the targets of student and community anger. Since this time, the government has attempted to find Blacks who are prepared to run the townships on its behalf. In 1977, the Community Councils Act was passed. This act set up government structures which were managed by elected representatives in the Black townships. Over the years, the government has attempted to strengthen the local authorities by giving them more powers.

As we saw earlier, the main weakness of these local authorities was that they depended on rents for their money. When they raised rents in the mid-1980s the communities rose in resistance. This resistance led to a challenge to the whole system of local authorities.

Most councillors fled the townships, rents were not collected and the whole system collapsed as councillors feared for their lives. In place of control by the Black Local Authorities, people in the townships began building street committees elected by the community.

The youth and communities also built 'people's courts'. These courts were supposed to replace 'apartheid justice' by 'people's justice'. The struggles against the local authorities resulted in violence and death as the youth and the communities clashed with the police and army.

Together, these political and economic aspects of the crisis left the government and the bosses searching for solutions. They made it clear however, that their idea of reform was very different to what trade unions and mass organisations were struggling for. This was especially because in order for the government to implement 'its reforms' it had to find some way to crush any serious opposition.

3. The Bosses and Government Fight Back

As the political and economic crisis escalated, the government saw that apartheid and capitalism could not be maintained in the old way. The government had to find new ways of maintaining apartheid and capitalism. The government offered two kinds of reform – political and economic.

Political Reforms

In response to the political crisis the government came up with the Tricameral Parliament. The Tricameral system gave the vote to the Coloured and Indian oppressed. The government made sure that its power would not be challenged, by having three separate 'chambers' for Whites, Coloureds and Indians. For the African oppressed the government introduced the Black Local Authorities. The government said that Africans could rule themselves in the townships with their Local Authorities. However, the community organisations and trade unions saw these government structures as an attempt to 'divide and rule'. The community organisations and trade unions called for a boycott of these bodies. As a result very few people voted for these bodies.

When the Tricameral Parliament and Black Local Authorities had failed in the period between 1984 and 1986, the bosses started looking for other solutions. Delegations of the bosses went to Lusaka to speak to the African National Congress (ANC). Their mission was to try and find political solutions acceptable to both capitalism and the ANC.

Some sections of the government, in alliance with the bosses, started looking at regional solutions. The most important of these was the Kwazulu-Natal Indaba, which brough Inkatha together with some of the White parliamentary parties in Natal.

The search for reforms has continued to be opposed by resistance from the masses. Certain sections in the government have also hindered this process. Now the government is talking about negotiating with all Black political groups, including those in exile, so long as those wishing to negotiate renounce violence. Most progressive organisations have rejected this government plan. They say that the government is simply trying to maintain minority rule. It is the apartheid system that is responsible for the violence in South Africa.

Economic Reforms

Most bosses felt that there were two main causes of the economic and political crisis. First, they felt that the government was too involved in the economy. They said that the government owned too many industries (like ISCOR and SASOL) and passed too many laws which controlled developments in industry. This made the industries political. For example any struggle against high electricity tariffs automatically became a struggle against the government because the government owns ESCOM.

Second, the bosses felt that part of the reason for the widespread dissatisfaction was that Blacks were denied business opportunities because of laws controlling their activities. They said that if Blacks felt part of the free enterprise system they would be satisfied. The bosses also said that inflation and the fiscal crisis was caused by the government spending too much money.

The government's economic reforms were a response to the crisis and to the way that the bosses viewed the crisis. The first solution proposed by the government was to sell off the companies owned by the state. This is called privatisation. Companies like the railways, SASOL, ISCOR, and so on are now being sold to the bosses.

The second solution was to pass laws that make it easy for Black businessmen to grow richer quickly. These laws also make it easy for those with small capital to enter business. This is called deregulation. Deregulation has also meant that those companies which have been deregulated can pay workers low wages. It also means terrible working conditions for workers. Trade unions have found struggles against such companies difficult because they are not covered by labour laws.

The whole of the government's economic reforms are guided by so-called free enterprise ideology. This ideology has been used by Thatcher in Britain and Reagan in America to crush trade unions. According to this ideology, trade unions are a problem because they prevent bosses from making high profits. According to Thatcher, when bosses are 'free' to make profits, it benefits everyone!

Because these political and economic reforms were challenged by the working class, the government was forced to turn to repression. For workers in South Africa free enterprise has meant more repression to allow the bosses to exploit!

The Road of Repression

From about 1985 the government was faced with a crisis which showed no signs of ending. The strategy of repression which had already started in 1984, was now intensified.

Troops Occupy the Townships

From 1984, the SADF occupied township after township as South Africa moved increasingly into a state of civil war. The increasing involvement of the SADF in the townships not only reflected the depth of the crisis, but also the growing power of the military in the government and all over South Africa. The age of the Generals had arrived!

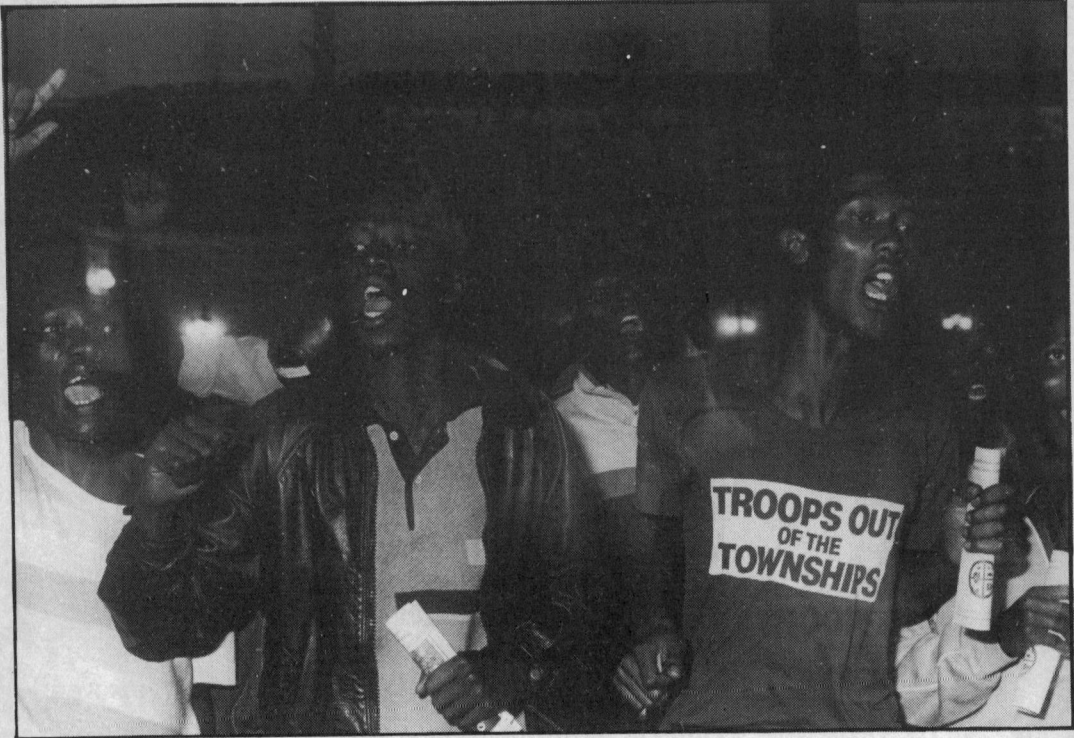

One of the important demands in the 1984-86 period was to get the troops out of the townships.

JMCs Take Control of the Townships

The power of the army in government was also reflected in the rise of the Joint Management Centres. These bodies are made up of all government departments active in a township plus certain 'important people' such as school principals and businessmen. These bodies were dominated by the police and army. They were responsible for crushing resistance in townships under their control. When the local authorities collapsed in a number of townships in the crisis period between 1984 and 1986, the JMCs took over. They were linked nationally through the National Security Management System.

The JMCs also co-ordinated strategies to crush the rent boycotts and schools boycotts. This involved evictions, the detention of activists, and the closure of schools. When such schools were reopened, activists were excluded.

Vigilantes

Another tactic of repression was the use of vigilantes to crush community organisations. The vigilantes were also used to carry out the forced removals. The government had found it difficult to remove some communities because of pressure from overseas and the resistance from the masses. Using vigilantes was also helpful to the government, because the government could make it appear as 'Black-on-Black' violence.

Leandra, January 1986. Members of the community defend themselves against vigilantes.

Detentions and Media Restrictions

In order to crush the mass resistance, the government detained thousands of activists for long periods. The government hoped that with the leadership detained, resistance might stop. At the same time the government imposed a number of restrictions on the media and on reportage of incidents of resistance.

States of Emergency

The detentions and vigilantes failed to halt the rising tide of mass resistance. To further weaken the mass movement, the government declared a State of Emergency over the whole country. This meant that organisations could no longer hold mass meetings. It also meant that mass funerals could no longer be held. The funerals were important political rallies in the period 1984 to 1986. The State of Emergency has been renewed every year and this has given the police and the military increased powers of repression.

Right-wing Death Squads

Over the past few years, many activists have been killed by secret death squads. These death squads have also burned and bombed the offices of progressive organisations and trade unions.

This tactic of death squads has been used a lot in South America. There the army dictatorships that rule don't use 'legal' means to crush the mass movement. South Africa is one of the few countries that have political and economic links with these countries.

The Banning of Organisations

When even the killing of activists failed to dampen mass resistance, the government banned the UDF and other mass organisations. It also restricted the activities of COSATU to economic issues on the factory floor.

The banning of organisations did not mean an end to the struggle, as the government had hoped.

More Restrictive Laws Passed

The government was still not satisfied with the repressive laws at its disposal. These laws did not seem to work. So it passed more repressive laws. The most important were the Labour Relations Amendment Act and the Education Act and a number of proclamations relating to education. These acts restricted the activities of workers and students and increased the power of the bosses and school authorities. Students could now be expelled if they were 'undesirable', which effectively meant students who continued the struggle against bantu education.

It was under these conditions that workers were forced to operate between 1984 and 1988. Despite their difficulties, and a number of setbacks, workers have continued to organise democratic trade unions and strive for unity to fight the power of the bosses and the government. We will discuss these struggles in the next chapter.

Chapter Fifteen
Workers Fight the Crisis

Workers have responded to the crisis by organising into massive trade union federations; especially COSATU and NACTU which have formed strong organisations and have developed clear political policies. It is on the basis of their strong organisation and clear political policies that the trade unions have been able to respond to the attacks of the government and the bosses.

This chapter is divided into the following sections:

1. **Trade Unions and Industrial Organisation**

2. **Trade Union Political Policy**

3. **The Living Wage Campaign**

4. **Unemployment and Co-operatives**

5. **Women, Culture, Health and Safety**

6. **The Labour Bill and Unity**

7. **Workers Forge Unity**

1. Trade Unions and Industrial Organisation

Since 1985, trade unions have grown in size and strength despite the bosses and government's attempts to smash them. By 1987 workers were taking strong militant action. Trade union membership rose rapidly and 9 million work days were lost as a result of worker action. The major developments since 1985 have been the strengthening of industrial unions through mergers and a clear formulation of political policies in the unions.

Cosatu affiliates worked hard during 1986 to put the slogan 'one industry, one union' into practice. By 1987, COSATU had grown into a massive federation representing 712 231 workers from twelve industrial unions. They were:

National Union of Mineworkers (NUM)	261 901
National Union of Metalworkers of South Africa (NUMSA)	130 796
Food and Allied Workers Union (FAWU)	65 278
Commercial, Catering and Allied Workers of South Africa (CCAWUSA)	56 000
South African Railways and Harbour Workers Union (SARHWU)	34 411
National Union of Textile Workers (NUTW)	30 538
Chemical Workers Industrial Union (CWIU)	29 859
Construction and Allied Workers Union (CAWU)	26 291
Paper Wood and Allied Workers Union (PWAWU)	23 310
Transport and General Workers Union (TGWU)	18 281
South African Mineworkers Union (SAMWU)	16 967
South African Domestic Workers Union (SADWU)	9 402
National Education, Health and Allied Workers Union (NEHAWU)	9 197

In October 1986, the Black consciousness trade unions also united. CUSA and AZACTU merged to form NACTU, which had over 400 000 members.

Twenty-four trade unions which affiliated to NACTU included:

Black Allied Mining and Construction Workers Union (BAMCWU)	4 119
Building, Construction and Allied Workers Union (BCAWU)	22 000
Food and Beverage Workers Union of South Africa (FBWU)	17 000
National Union of Wine, Spirit and Allied Workers (NUWSAW)	4 881
South African Chemical Workers Union (SACWU)	32 000
Steel, Engineering and Allied Workers Union (SEAWU)	5 500
Transport and Allied Workers Union (TAWU)	8 000
United African Motor and Allied Workers Union (UAMAWU)	8 000

By the time of their second congress, NACTU membership had dropped substantially. Their official figure at the congress was 169 485. After the congress, NACTU held a press conference in which it stated that its three strongest unions are the South African Chemical Workers Union, the Building, Construction and Allied Workers Union and the Food and Beverage Workers Union. Other trade unions like the Textile Workers Union have as few as 400 members.

NACTU also encouraged its affiliates, like the five different affiliates in the metal and motor industry, to merge into strong industrial unions.

Many trade unions also remained independent. Some of these affiliates worked closely with COSATU affiliates on specific campaigns. While others, like GAWU, have been involved in merger talks. GAWU plans to merge with ACTWUSA in September 1989.

While great strides have been made in forming one union for each industry, this goal is still a long way off. Unity has often been hindered by the different political policies adopted by the large federations and independent unions. These policies have emerged in the course of struggle and at the various union congresses held around the country.

NEHAWU delegates at the COSATU Second Congress

2. Trade Union Policy

COSATU held its second congress in Johannesburg in 1987. 1 438 delegates representing 712 231 workers from twelve industrial unions attended the congress. Unions within COSATU fiercely debated political policy at their union congresses, decided on policy, and took their positions forward to the COSATU congress. At times, the debates within and between the affiliates led to serious differences.

Eventually, the congress passed the following resolutions which built on earlier resolutions and policies:

- It adopted the **Freedom Charter** as a guiding document in the struggle and agreed to develop a united working class understanding of its demands.
- It encouraged COSATU and all progressive organisations to discuss socialism and democracy.
- It resolved to remain politically independent, but to develop disciplined and structured alliances with progressive organisations at the local, regional and national levels.
- It supported comprehensive and mandatory sanctions, and called for the complete isolation of the South African state, businessmen and sports players.
- It encouraged trade unions which support its principles to join COSATU on the basis of 'One Union, One Industry'.

COSATU members relied on these policies when they formed alliances with political organisations, and participated in joint mass action with the UDF and the NECC. COSATU's call was 'Forward to Mass Action'.

At its launching congress, NACTU stated its working principles of worker control, Black working class leadership, non-affiliation to political organisations, financial accountability and union independence within NACTU policy.

NACTU resolutions committed the federation to anti-capitalism, anti-imperialism, anti-racism, and anti-sexism. NACTU argued for co-operation with organisations committed to the same goals, to develop a system of alternative education, to fight women's oppression, to support full sanctions until apartheid and capitalism end.

At its annual congress in 1988, NACTU developed its policies further. It dropped the principle of 'Black working class' leadership for the principle of 'African working class' leadership. It argued that the term African stood for all those fighting for a free Azania.

NACTU also passed resolutions on the following:

- to continue supporting all liberation movements in South Africa
- that Azania belongs only to African people
- that the struggle is also for the repossession of conquered land
- to work towards one country, one federation by setting up working relationships with COSATU
- the need to launch a national campaign to include farmworkers and domestic workers under the Labour Relations Acts
- NACTU affiliates be urged to form Women's Committees.

Although the large federations had some differences, it was clear that they were also united around a number of similar issues and against the exploitation and oppression of working men and women. But resolutions are only important when they are put into practice. The trade union campaigns were very important in building unity and fighting the power of the bosses and the government.

3. The Living Wage Campaign

Faced with rising inflation and starvation wages, workers throughout South Africa have been fighting bitter battles with the bosses for higher wages and decent living standards. Workers in COSATU, in NACTU and in some of the independent unions have been fighting for these rights.

COSATU Living Wage Campaign

COSATU affiliates believe that every worker has a right to a living wage and COSATU launched a campaign to fight for this right. Under the leadership of COSATU, millions of workers, women and youth stand united in the fight for a living wage and a decent life.

The main demands of the COSATU Living Wage Campaign:

- a guaranteed annual income
- a living wage
- a 40 hour week
- no tax deductions
- job security
- March 21, May 1 and June 16 as paid public holidays
- retrenchment pay of one months salary for every year of employment
- six months paid maternity leave and job guaranteed
- increased vocational training for women and youth
- decent education and training
- an end to the hostel system and decent housing near work
- the right to picket

The Living Wage Campaign was meant to be co-ordinated by a National Co-ordinating Committee (NCC) and Regional Co-ordinating Committees. Unfortunately these committees were never established because COSATU structures were not strong enough to take up this campaign. COSATU locals were also meant to play a central role by educating and mobilising workers to support the campaign.

The COSATU Living Wage Campaign faced many difficulties as well as the full force of state repression. But this did not mean that workers did not continue the struggle for a living wage.

257

CCAWUSA

From December 1986 to February 1987, 10 000 OK workers fought for a living wage. Workers from all OK branches in South Africa, united, went on strike and said, 'We will not work until you pay us a living wage.'

'Striking at Gold' – The 1987 Mineworkers Strike

The strike by about 340 000 mineworkers in August 1987, was the biggest and most expensive wage strike in the history of South Africa. The mines are the backbone of South African capitalism, yet workers in this industry are still struggling for a living wage and safer working conditions. At the time of the strike, the lowest paid workers earned R230 per month on the gold mines and R335 per month on the coal mines.

NUM workers ballot to shake the Chamber of Mines in 1987.

The strike lasted 21 days. Management used many strike breaking tactics. They blocked officials from the mines, prevented workers from holding meetings, threatened to evict workers from hostels and cut off their food supplies. Mine security and the police assaulted and detained many workers. On the 12 August the entire committee of the Klerksdorp region was arrested. Strike leadership was removed from Carltonville, Westonaria, Witbank and the Orange Free State region.

Metal Unions Unite for a Living Wage

In 1988 metalworkers came together for the first time in a joint campaign for annual wage negotiations. The four unions that took part in the campaign are NUMSA, SEAWUSA (Steel Engineering and Allied Workers Union of South Africa), EAWU (Engineering and Allied Workers Union) and EAWTUSA (Electrical and Allied Workers Trade Union of South Africa). This was also the first time that workers and unions from COSATU and NACTU united to present workers' demands to the bosses in wage negotiations.

SARHWU

On 12 March 1987, a SARHWU member was dismissed from SATS. Railway workers in over 250 depots joined in solidarity action and demanded the recognition of SARHWU. Throughout the strike, SATS management refused to negotiate with SARHWU and tried to bolster their 'sweetheart' union*, BLATU.

sweetheart union – a trade union which supports the policies of management and discourages workers from taking militant action to fight for their rights.

The South African Police responded by trying to put an end to the strike. It broke up SARHWU meetings, held COSATU House under siege and seven railway workers were shot. The government also used the SATS strike to launch a massive propaganda campaign against COSATU. Police raided COSATU and its affiliates' offices, and the Living Wage Campaign and May Day rallies throughout South Africa were banned.

SATS management was eventually forced to negotiate with SARHWU. None of the 18 000 members lost their jobs, and SATS was eventually forced to recognise SARHWU.

NACTU Fights for Farmworkers

More than 1 200 farmworkers attended the inaugural congress of the National Union of Farmworkers (NUF) on the 28 February 1988. The objective of the NUF is to unite farmworkers to challenge their exclusion from the Labour Relations Act. NUF is the largest farmworkers' union in the country.

Since its formation, the NUF has signed agreements covering wage negotiations and working conditions with many companies. It has also begun to take up the struggles of farmworkers. About 100 NUF members were dismissed while on strike at Impala Nurseries in Magaliesburg. Workers went on strike on 14 April 1988 in demand of wage increases, better working conditions, and the recognition of their union. The farmer at Impala has applied successfully to the Supreme Court to have workers evicted from the farm by 18 June 1988.

SACWU Fights for Chemical Workers

On October 1 South African Chemical Workers Union (SACWU) members in Sasol 1 went on a strike for higher wages. Two days after the strike began, Sasol management evicted workers from the hostels. Workers were also harassed by local council police and vigilantes who attacked them in the hostels.

POTWA Strike

Between August 3 and September 3 1988, 21 000 postal workers throughout South Africa went on strike. They were striking against racial discrimination, lack of parity in wages and working status, and the lack of meaningful structures of communication in the Post Office.

POTWA workers strike against the Post Office, 1987.

Management responded by dismissing 3 000 workers, and refused to negotiate an end to the strike. The Post Office was eventually forced to negotiate, when the Postal Telegraph and Telephone International threatened to disrupt South Africa's communication links.

The strike came to an end after negotiations with the Postmaster General and POTWA. Dismissed workers could apply for reinstatement within seven days, workers won wage increases and a joint management board of review was appointed to look into the question of parity.

Management only re-employed 1 400 of the 3 000 dismissed workers, and these were mostly only skilled workers.

These were just a few of the many strikes by workers since 1985. They showed that workers were determined to challenge the capitalists and cheap labour and to struggle for a living wage. Although some of the strikes ended in victory, workers also learnt the lesson that the bosses had the power to dismiss workers even if they organised a legal strike. The NUM was especially hard hit when the bosses dismissed over 50 000 workers during the mineworkers strike!

4. Unemployment and Co-operatives

With the increasing numbers of unemployed, trade unions realised that they had to assist the unemployed and dismissed workers.

COSATU has set up the National Unemployed Workers Co-ordinating Committee which co-ordinates groups of unemployed workers in the struggle against unemployment.

COSATU has also begun to organise the unemployed into co-operatives and NACTU passed a resolution in 1988 to set up a co-operative unit. At present COSATU unions organising co-operatives include NUMSA, NUM, and ACTWUSA. In a co-op unemployed workers can earn some money and learn important skills. Co-operatives also help to build and maintain democratic worker organisation.

The Sarmcol Workers Co-op

When 960 BTR Sarmcol workers were dismissed in 1985, their union MAWU, set up the SARMCOL Workers Co-operative (SAWCO) to keep workers united.

SAWCO is divided into different projects:

- The Bulk Buying Project distributes food parcels to strikers and their families.
- The Agriculture Project grows vegetables.

SAWCO workers growing their own vegetables.

- The T-shirt Project prints designs on t-shirts for unions and progressive organisations.
- The Health Project monitors the health of the strikers and their families.
- The Culture Project produces plays which are used to spread the story of the Sarmcol struggle.

SAWCO project members come together in a Membership General Meeting which is the highest decision making body of SAWCO. SAWCO workers are still linked to their union NUMSA, through local and regional structures.

In the Eastern Cape, NUMSA has also been organising co-operatives. The co-ops started with initiatives from NAAWU. The NAAWU National Executive Council decided to start a co-operative building project called the Co-operative Centre, in which NUMSA and other unions in Port Elizabeth will have offices. NUMSA also hopes to start a co-op supermarket in a warehouse.

ACTWUSA

ACTWUSA is setting up a co-op, called Zenzeleni, for retrenched Frame workers. It is a cut, sew and trim co-op in which about 1 000 workers will work. The co-op will operate as a factory controlled by a governing body of trustees which has a majority of ACTWUSA office bearers. Worker representatives and management sit on a Board of Directors. The union has hired skilled management who will administer the factory. Shop stewards, together with workers will ensure that all decisions are carried out. The factory will pay wages determined by the Industrial Council.

NUM

When workers were dismissed in Phalaborwa in 1986, NUM set up a t-shirt co-op. The 88 workers in the co-op got a capital grant to start the co-op. Since then, they have received no subsidies and live on what they produce. The surplus they make is divided into the number of hours worked.

NUM has also used its relief fund to set up co-ops in the Transkei and in Lesotho. Dismissed migrant workers work in the co-ops. In the Transkei, NUM has two co-ops, which organise workers from 28 districts and one in Lesotho. Each project in the Transkei has 63 members. The co-ops make concrete building blocks. Sixty-three members belong to the Lesotho co-op. Workers make 1 500 building blocks a day.

The struggle to organise the unemployed, dismissed and retrenched workers is a big task. However trade unions have realised that the struggle of the unemployed is a struggle for the working class as a whole.

Women make up at least half of the working class. Women workers suffer exploitation and oppression in the home, at work and in the community. Despite this, the trade unions in South Africa have been slow to organise women. But women are beginning to organise and have shown the union federations their strength.

5. Women, Culture, Health and Safety

COSATU Women's Congress

In order to begin taking up women's struggles in COSATU, COSATU held a Women's Congress in April 1988. Between 22 and 24 April 1988, over 300 women from unions in COSATU came together to discuss their problems as women. Representatives from women's organisations like FEDTRAW (Federation of Transvaal Women), and NOW (Natal Organisation of Women) also attended the conference.

COSATU women debated what was happening to them at work, in their unions and in their communities. They eventually decided to take up women's struggles in COSATU by forming women's forums at a local level.

The COSATU Women's Congress, 1988

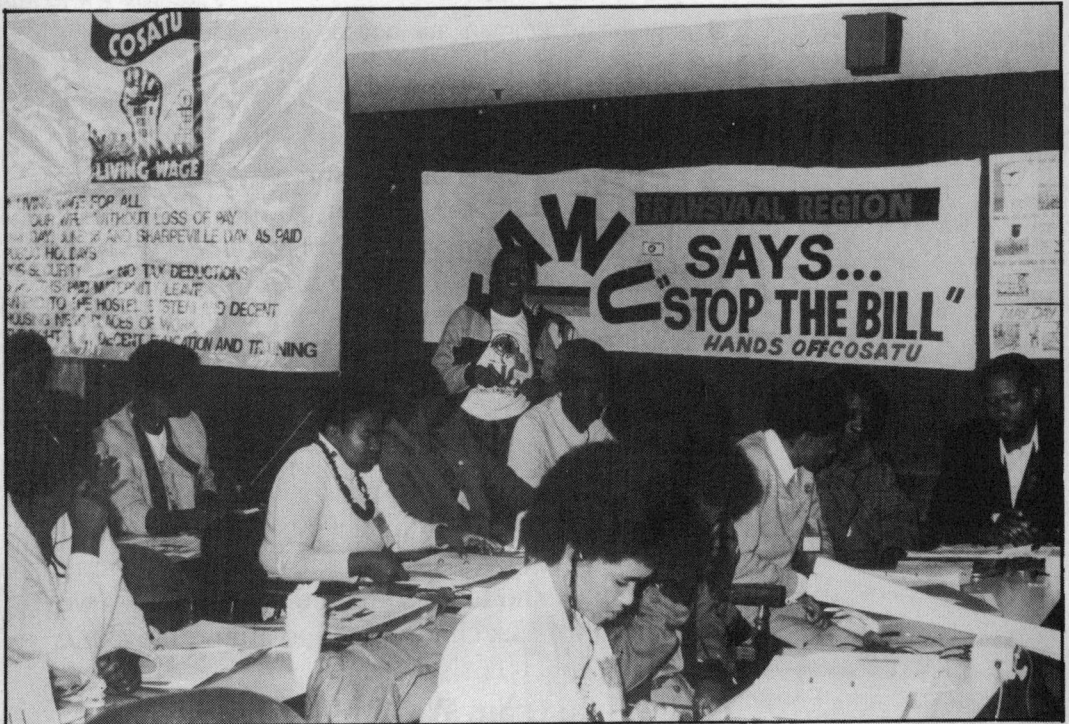

At the COSATU Women's Congress women demanded:

- that COSATU educate its membership so that men and women can have equal relationships at home, at work and in politics;

- that COSATU educate its members about rape and train women in self defence so that they can defend themselves against attacks by men;

- that COSATU fight with other organisations for the right to a safe, free and legal abortion whenever women want it;

- that women discuss how they face sexual harassment from men in the union, at work and in the community;

- at least nine months paid maternity leave;

- paid time off to attend the clinic;

- free, safe contraception and proper sex education for all;

- safe working conditions;

- that domestic workers and farm workers should also get UIF;

- that the government and bosses provide free child care.

Many unions in Cosatu have taken the women's struggle forward. They have won maternity leave agreements from the bosses, and have organised women's forums in their unions so that women can begin to fight against their oppression. MAWU, now NUMSA, won six months paid maternity leave for its members at a national level, during wage negotiations in 1986. This is a small victory in terms of job security and pay for women when they are pregnant. CCAWUSA won an even bigger battle in 1988 when it won a parental rights agreement with Pick 'n Pay. This parental rights agreement makes it possible for women and men to combine holding a job with a normal family life. The agreement, grants mothers eleven months leave and fathers eighteen days leave as well as time off for sick children and to attend the clinic.

NACTU takes up Women's Demands

NACTU set up the Women's Unit to support NACTU policy on women. The Women's Unit has conducted

seminars for and assisted the affiliates with
information for negotiation on women's issues at the
workplace.

The Women's Unit has produced booklets on:

- Equality of opportunity for women in the workplace
- Workplace hazards and women workers
- Effective collective bargaining clauses for union women
- Maternity benefits

Culture

Many cultural groups have developed in COSATU.
Workers in these groups have produced plays, songs
and poetry which speak of workers' oppression and
their courageous struggles against capitalism and
apartheid. A Cultural Day was held at the COSATU
second congress, at which workers shared their
cultural work.

*The Long March – SARMCOL workers share their struggles in this
play.*

COSATU has set up a culture unit to take workers' struggles in culture forward. The role of the Culture Unit is to encourage worker participation around culture, conduct workshops with cultural groups within COSATU, and build other cultural units.

Health and Safety

Increasingly workers have been challenging the bosses over their right to make decisions about health and safety. Workers are saying that it is their lives that are at stake and that they have the right to health and safety. COSATU unions are demanding 'Health before profits'.

6. The Labour Bill and Unity

In September 1987 the bosses and the government introduced the new Labour Bill. The Minister of Manpower said that the bill would 'hang like a sword over the heads of the unions'. The bill was the bosses' and their government's answer to the militant struggles of organised workers and especially to COSATU's Living Wage Campaign.

As the trade union federations grew in strength and clearly voiced their opposition to apartheid and capitalism, they came under increasing repression and attack from the state. Trade union offices are constantly raided and unionists detained and harassed. During 1986, COSATU House was bombed and destroyed. Other trade union offices have been repeatedly raided and even fire bombed. Unionists also now have to face the actions of vigilantes in the townships.

The aim of the bill was to attack workers' main weapons of struggle – strikes, solidarity strikes, blocking actions and boycotts; to attack workers' organisation; to attack workers' legal rights by making unfair dismissals and retrenchments legal, and by letting the government minister decide what an unfair labour practice is.

COSATU House under siege by the state

The bosses supported the new bill. COSATU condemned it as a fundamental attack on the trade union movement. COSATU affiliates showed their rejection of the bill by holding lunch-time factory demonstrations, holding meetings with the bosses at factory, industry and national levels and by sending a letter to all the bosses calling on them to reject the bill.

In response to these attacks 1 500 delegates from COSATU's thirteen affiliates met to discuss the government's restrictions on COSATU and the Labour Bill. 'Taken together, the bill and restrictions effectively ban COSATU,' said Jay Naidoo the general secretary.

120 delegates representing UDF affiliates, church and sports organisations, all with full speaking rights, attended the COSATU Special Congress.

A lot of discussion and debate took place at the congress. To show their rejection of the Labour Bill, the restrictions on COSATU's political activity, and the banning of the UDF and sixteen other organisations, workers decided to have three days of peaceful protest action and to form a 'broad alliance of forces' committed to the removal of apartheid.

Stayaway June 6, 7 and 8

The protest action on the sixth, seventh and eighth of June was a huge success. Not only did the majority of the working class stay away from work, but organisations within the working class began to show greater unity. COSATU held discussions with NACTU, and various community and student groups, who supported the three day action. This was the biggest, strongest and longest protest action in the history of the struggle in South Africa.

Millions of workers showed their rejection of the bill by staying away from work. About 75% of workers, (almost 3 million workers) throughout the country stayed away over the three days. This led to a R500 million loss for capital. For the first time in the history of South Africa, the bosses felt the power of the united working class.

Soweto bus and taxi station – deserted during the stayaway of 6, 7 and 8 June 1988

The bosses and the government were forced to listen to workers' demands after the stayaway. In the middle of the protest, the government minister said his door was open to discuss the bill. The bosses' organisation, SACCOLA, said they wanted to negotiate with COSATU about the bill and reach 'agreement' on workers' objections to the bill.

COSATU and NACTU began negotiations with SACCOLA in June 1988 over workers' objections to the bill. But this was all a waste of time because in August 1988, the government informed COSATU and SACCOLA that the Labour Bill would become law on the 1 September 1988.

7. Workers Forge Unity

Trade union federations and progressive organisations have begun to realise the need to build greater unity. COSATU has begun to build this unity through the Anti-apartheid Conference and the Workers' Summit.

Anti-Apartheid Conference

The COSATU Special Congress decided that a special conference organising committee made up of COSATU (CEC) and its allies would plan and host a conference. The committee's task was to develop a programme of action against repression, and to hold an 'Anti-apartheid Conference' where a wide range of organisations could discuss the new Labour Law, the banning of political organisations and the October municipal elections, and how workers could respond to these issues.

COSATU members debated who should participate in the broad alliance and how many delegates would be allowed. But the government responded by banning the planned conference and placing severe restrictions on many worker leaders.

The Workers' Summit

On 3 and 4 March 1989, COSATU, independent unions and eleven NACTU affiliates attended a workers' summit in Johannesburg. 42 trade unions and six observers attended the conference. The summit was held to push for greater unity amongst the working class and for workers to show their united rejection of the Labour Relations Act.

The NACTU affiliates attending the conference included the Food and Beverage Workers Union (FBWU), Black Electronics and Electrical Workers Union, Brushes and Cleaners Workers Union, Banking Insurance and Finance Assurance Workers Union, Black Domestic Workers Association, SA Laundry Dry-Cleaning and Dyeing Workers Union, Black Allied Mining and Construction Workers Union (BAMCWU), National Union of Public Service Workers, Natal Liquor and Catering Trades Employees Union, Electrical and Allied Workers Trade Union.

The unions attended despite NACTU's leadership call for the summit to be indefinitely postponed. The NACTU affiliates stated that they attended because they wanted to show their commitment to 'the maximum unity of the working class'.

The independent unions included:

- Orange Vaal General Workers Union (OVGWU)
- Durban Integrated Employees Society
- Electricity Workers Union
- Garment and Allied Workers Union
- National Union of Brick & and Allied Workers
- South African Wood Workers Union
- University of Western Cape Workers Union
- Zakheni Transport and Allied Workers Union
- SA Postal Telecommunications Employees Union

- Engineering and Industrial Workers Union
- National Workers Union of South Africa
- SA Post Office Employees Association
- National Union of Steel and Allied Workers
- Combined Small Factory Workers Union
- African Mineworkers Union

Workers decided to formulate their own Labour Relations Act (LRA).

Workers demanded:
- the right to strike and picket;
- no dismissals without proper hearings;
- retrenchments must be negotiated with trade unions and conducted in accordance with the 'first in, last out' principle;
- only majority unions should be recognised;
- the right to sympathy strikes.

The unions also agreed that farmworkers, forestry workers, public sector workers and domestic workers should be covered by the Labour Relations Act and that unions should avoid using the Industrial Court and rather use independent arbitration or mediation to resolve disputes.

Workers gave employers 30 days to begin meeting their demands and for the Labour Relations Act to be scrapped. If employers failed to do so, the unions attending the summit would declare a national dispute with all bosses. Workers agreed to isolate bosses who use the LRA against unions. This might include their products being boycotted nationally and internationally.

Habe! The struggle of workers for trade unions in South Africa has come a long way.

Workers have fought bitter battles against the bosses and the government. But through fighting these battles, they have learnt the importance of unity. Today, many more workers than ever before in South Africa are organised into trade unions. The membership of COSATU stands at 715 000 and that of NACTU at 170 000. But thousands of workers still remain unorganised. The majority of the unemployed are also unorganised.

But workers in trade unions are taking their struggle forward. In March 1989 many trade unions met at a workers' summit to organise to fight the bosses' and the government's newest weapon: the Labour Relations Act. But unity between the trade union federations is still a long way off.

Workers have also begun to find ways of fighting for their political rights. They have begun building unity between trade unions and other progressive organisations. But the bosses, the government and their allies continue to do everything in their power to crush this growing power. They continue to ban organisations, detain our leaders and restrict their movements. The bosses and government have also used vigilantes to divide workers and attack their organisations in the factories and in the townships.

But we know them better now. Whatever they do, we know they can't stop our struggle for Freedom from Below!

The Struggle Continues!
Freedom or Death!
Victory is Certain!

ACKNOWLEDGEMENTS

Many publications were used in the writing and production of this book. We take this opportunity to apologise to those whose rights may have been unwittingly infringed. We hope that they have furthered the cause of expanding the availability of knowledge to all people in South Africa. Pictures, graphics and other information were taken from the following.

Gavin Brown — *Hard Labour* IR Data Publications 1978

Luli Callinicos — *A People's History of South Africa: Gold and Workers 1886 – 1924* Ravan Press 1985

Luli Callinicos — *A People's History of South Africa: Working Life 1886 – 1940, Factories, Townships and Popular Culture on the Rand* Ravan Press 1987

Jeremy Cronin and Raymond Suttner — *30 Years of the Freedom Charter* Ravan Press 1986

D. Denoon — *Southern Africa since 1800* Longman 1972

Bill Freund — *The Making of Contemporary Africa* MacMillan Press 1984

Steven Friedman — *Building Tomorrow Today: African Workers in Trade Unions 1970 – 1984* Ravan Press 1986

Nicholas Haysom — *Mabangalala: The Rise of Right-wing Vigilantes in South Africa* Centre for Applied Legal Studies 1986

Norman Herd — *1922 – The Revolt on the Rand* Blue Crane Books 1966

Duncan Innes — *Anglo American and the Rise of Modern South Africa* Ravan Press 1984

H. Wynn Jones — *Africa in Perspective* Quadriga Press 1960

T. Karis and G.M. Carter — *From Protest to Challenge. A Documentary History of African Politics in South Africa 1882 – 1964* Volumes 1, 2, 4 Hoover Institution Press 1972

G.H. Le May — *Black and White in South Africa, The Politics of Survival* Purnall and Sons Ltd. 1971

John Lewis — *Industrialisation and Trade Union Organisation in South Africa, 1924 – 1955. The Rise and Fall of the South African Trades and Labour Council* Cambridge University Press 1984

Tom Lodge — *Black Politics in South Africa Since 1945* Ravan Press 1983

Denis MacShane, Martin Plaut, David Ward — *Power! Black Workers, their unions and the struggle for Freedom in South Africa* Spokesman 1984

Shamim Marie — *Divide and Profit: Indian Workers in Natal* Worker Resistance and Culture Publications 1986

Don Ncube — *Black Trade Unions in South Africa* Skotaville Publishers 1985

Robert F. Osborn — *Valiant Harvest* South African Sugar Association 1964

Vishnu Padayachee, Shahid Vawda and Paul Tichmann — *Indian Workers and Trade Unions in Durban: 1930 to 1950* Institute for Social and Economic Research 1985

Neil Parsons — *A New History of Southern Africa* MacMillan Press 1982

Henry R. Pike — *A History of Communism in South Africa* Christian Mission International of South Africa 1985

Ambrose Reeves — *Shooting at Sharpeville: The Agony of South Africa* Victor Gollancz 1960

Brian Roberts — *Kimberley: Turbulent City* David Philip 1976

Edward Roux — *Time Longer than Rope: The Black Man's Struggle for Freedom in South Africa* University of Wisconsin Press 1978 edition

Keith Sorrenson — *Separate and Unequal* Heinemann Educational Books 1976

Peter Walshe — *The Rise of African Nationalism in South Africa. The African National Congress 1912 – 1952*

I.L. Walker and B. Weinbren — *A History of the South African Labour Movement. 2 000 Casualties* South African Trade Union Council 1961

Eddie Webster — *Cast in a Racial Mould: Labour Process and Trade Unions in the Foundry* Ravan Press 1985

P.L. Wickens — *The Industrial and Commercial Workers Union of South Africa* Oxford University Press 1978

Institute for Industrial Education — *The Durban Strikes 1973* Institute for Industrial Education and Ravan Press 1974

South African Institute of Race Relations — *Race Relations Survey:* various issues

South African Research Service — *South African Review* Volumes 1 – 3; Ravan Press 1983 – 1986

South African Labour Bulletin Volume 1: various issues

Africa Perspective: various issues

State of the Nation: various issues

Weekly Mail: various issues

Work in Progress: various issues

Various trade union newspapers, reports and publications

Thanks to COSATU Resources and Billy Paddock for some pictures.

Picture Acknowledgements

The visual material in this book derives from a number of sources. While every effort has been made to trace the owners of copyright, this has not always been possible. We offer our apologies to anyone whose rights we have unwittingly infringed.

AFRAPIX: Paul Weinberg 189, 236, 245, 253, 263, 267; Anna Zieminski 239, 270; Eric Miller 257(top), 258, 269; Santu Mofokeng 247, 261, 265; Gisele Wulfson 244; Chris Ledochowski 257(bottom).

Gavin Browne *Hard Labour I.R.D.* Data Publications, 1985: 203.

L. Callinicos *A People's History of South Africa: Working Life 1886-1940, Factories, Townships and Popular Culture on the Rand* Ravan Press, 1981: 91.

L. Callinicos *A People's History of South Africa: Gold and Workers 1886-1924* Ravan Press, 1985: 20, 24, 35, 38, 39, 41.

Cape Town Library: 66.

Mrs Bob Connolly: 82.

Community Resources Information Centre (CRIC) *May Day Booklet*, 1938: 87.

COSATU Booklet: 229, 231.

COSATU Print Unit Collection: 182, 186, 188, 192, 208, 224.

Jeremy Cronin and Raymond Suttner: *30 Years of the Freedom Charter* Ravan Press, 1986: 146, 217.

Daily News, Durban, 1973: 166.

The Garment Worker/Die Klerewerker: 85.

Industrial Development in South Africa 1904-05: 50, 78, 84.

International Defence and Aid Fund for Southern Africa: 79, 103, 141, 143, 145.

K. Luckhardt: *Organise or Starve: The History of the South African Congress of Trade Unions* Lawrence and Wishart, 1980: 99, 116, 121, 125, 128, 130, 131.

Mandlenkosi Makhoba *The Sun Shall Rise for Workers* Ravan Press, 1984: 176.

Natal Mercury: 162, 164.

S. Nzima: 180.

SAR Magazine, 1905-36: 21, 32, 55, 60.

SARMCOL: 223.

SASPU National/ Work in Progress: 220.

The Star Archives: 102.

Stewart, Cape Town: 67.

Strange Memorial Library: 68.

Petrus Tom *My Life Struggle* Ravan Press, 1985: 172.

H. Wynn Jones *Africa in Perspective* Quadriga Press, 1960: 56.

Trade Union Addresses

COSATU Head Office
6th Floor
National Acceptances House
cnr Rissik & Anderson Streets
Johannesburg
2001

ACTWUSA Head Office
68 Blake Road
Durban
4001

CAWU Head Office
68 Von Wielligh Street
Johannesburg
2001

CCAWUSA Head Office
7th Floor
Park Chambers
8 Wanderers Street
Johannesburg
2001

CWIU Head Office
5 Eaton Road
Congella
Durban
4001

FAWU Head Office
355 Albert Road
Woodstock
7935

GAWU Head Office
Industria House
350 Victory Road
Salt River
7925

NEHAWU Head Office
502 Queens Court
3 Klein Street
Johannesburg
2001

NUM Head Office
5th Floor
National Acceptances House
cnr Rissik & Anderson Streets
Johannesburg
2001

NUMSA Head Office
3rd Floor
National Acceptances House
cnr Rissik & Anderson Streets
Johannesburg
2001

NUWCC Head Office
214 2nd Floor Darragh House
13 Wanderers Street
Johannesburg
2001

POTWA Head Office
1st Floor
Darragh House
13 Wanderers Street
Johannesburg
2001

PPWAWU Head Office
2nd Floor
Fillian Building
Becker Street
Johannesburg
2000

SADWU Head Office
Community House
41 Salt River Road
Salt River
7925

SAMWU Head Office
Trade Union House
8 Beverley Street
Athlone
7764

SARHWU Head Office
2nd Floor
Metropolitan Building
16 President Street
Johannesburg
2001

T & GWU Head Office
7th Floor
Pasteur Chambers
Jeppe Street
Johannesburg
2001